PRAISE FOR *THE BIG TRIP: A FAMILY GAP YEAR*

Martha McManamy has written a fascinating chronicle of the year spent with her three teenage children traveling through Spain, Kenya, Guatemala and Bolivia where they lived with families and offered volunteer service. The fun, caring relations they developed with each other and the people they encountered filled me with admiration and hope, knowing these young people will continue to live as caring citizens of the world. **–Barbara Hildt, former Massachusetts State Representative and Peace Corps volunteer**

The Big Trip thoughtfully shows readers how opening up to the bigger world actually can bring families closer. I really enjoyed the sharing of practical considerations to see how the McManamy family made the extensive overseas stay work, as well as the contributions from the children. **–Homa S. Tavangar, Author,** *Growing Up Global: Raising Children to Be At Home in the World*

Martha McManamy offers a fascinating story that gives parents of teens (and students themselves!) great inspiration to plan and implement their own grand adventure. With humor and warmth, she explores both the challenges and the delights of shepherding young almost-adults through experiences that help them grow as individuals and citizens of the world. Thanks to her, more parents will choose to take their kids on a truly mind-enriching and heart-opening journey abroad. **–Maya Frost,** *The New Global Student*

A captivating travel memoir! This inspirational book shows that teens can learn far more "on the road" than they ever could in a classroom, whilst forging friendships and family memories that will last a lifetime. The world would be a more tolerant, peaceful place in which to live if more families would pick up on their lead. **–Christine Stewart, President, Stewart International, Ltd.**

This is a great account of one family's admirable decision to replace the traditional learning/working trajectory with an experiential one and immerse themselves in the uncertainty of the world waiting for them. **–Kristin Houk, President and CEO, NamasteDirect**

To Kay and Martin,
and

THE
BIG
TRIP

A Family Gap Year

Joyful journeys,
Love,
Martha McManamy

Martha McManamy with
Evan, Conor,
and Laura McManamy

ISBN: 978-1-4834-1402-7 (sc)
ISBN: 978-1-4834-1401-0 (e)

Library of Congress Control Number: 2014910767

Because of the dynamic nature of the Internet, any web addresses or links contained in this book may have changed since publication and may no longer be valid. The views expressed in this work are solely those of the author and do not necessarily reflect the views of the publisher, and the publisher hereby disclaims any responsibility for them.

Lulu Publishing Services rev. date: 7/3/2014

TABLE OF CONTENTS

GRATITUDE

A web of connections has been built consisting of deep friendships across the miles. I am grateful to these new friends and to many more whom we met along the way who have left impressions but not their names. **France:** Rebecca, Bernard and JR in Toulouse; Karina and Gen in Anglars-Juillac. **Spain:** Nuria, Pep, Victor, Marina and Alba in Barcelona; Adolfo and Gemma in Sueca; Conchita, Juan and Elena in Almuñecar; Manolo, Asunción, Manuel, Fabiola and Jesus, in Madrid. **Morocco:** Laure, Wafa, Najib, Leila and Souki in Mohammedia; Karina and Ahmed in Marrakech; Rachid at Gite Tizi N'Oucheg; Brahim in Casablanca; Elias in Rabat. **Kenya:** Peter and Margaret, and Father Dick in Nairobi; Eden, Jim, Isaiah and Jesse of Friends United Meeting in Kisumu; Dorothy, Father Ida, Ray and Sukie of Kakamega Children's Care Centre; Moses and Bernadette in Kakamega; Sherry and Priscilla in Esabalu; Mark and Katie of Amesbury for Africa. **Guatemala:** Saskia of AVP Friends Peace Teams; Deet and Margaret in Antigua; Teresa of Open Windows in San Miguel Dueñas; Bob, Kristin and Jaime of Namaste Direct in Antigua; Juan Pablo of Los Patojos in Jocotenango; Elizabeth (founder of Long Way Home), Flavio and Amarildo in San Juan Comalapa; Dave and Kathy (founders of Safe Stoves) with Pop Wuj Language School, Quetzaltenango. **Bolivia:** Bernabé, Juan, Ruben, Alicia, Judith, and Newton of the Bolivia Quaker Education Fund in La Paz; Barbara, Eusebio and Maria of the Hogar in Sorata; Ninfa, Hans, Rebecca and Johan of the Congregación Cristiana Amigos in Cochabamba; Luis and Marta in La Paz. **Argentina:** Monica, Lucas, and Claudio in Buenos Aires. You have all taught us so much, and we are forever grateful for your friendship.

I thank my children, Evan, Conor, and Laura, for their companionship, their trust, and for not complaining. Even the first step would not have been taken without the support and encouragement of John, my co-traveler and keeper of the home fires.

JUMPING OFF

"Travel is fatal to prejudice, bigotry and
narrow-mindedness." Mark Twain

"To be bored of traveling is an oxymoron!" Conor McManamy

It was mainly about holding my teenage kids tight before letting
them go. As teenage years approached, I had been achingly
conscious that soon my three would move out, that our years of
living together would come to a screeching halt. I remembered
my own parents feeling the same way so many years before when
I blithely skipped off to college and beyond. The plan was to slow
down the treadmill, that conveyor belt that moves inexorably from
kindergarten to college and then to the expectation of a lifetime
of employment.

The kids were just excited about taking a year off from school, a
gap year. Who wouldn't want to play hooky? They looked forward
to having adventures and visiting places that none of us had ever
seen. The timing worked out well for all of them. Evan, the eldest,
would be entering college when we returned. The twins, Conor

and Laura, would be starting high school. Since they were all moving to different schools, leaving friends was less of a concern than it might have been otherwise. And it was hard to turn down a fabulous adventure. We had traveled in the developing world before, so we knew we were capable of leaving behind the comforts of home.

So we decided to take a Big Trip together. I would take a year off my consulting gig and be the primary tour director and guide. My husband, John, would join us several times over the year when he was able to get away. He deserved a halo for his attitude about the Big Trip. Unable to take a full year off, he could join us only when his vacation schedule allowed, and even then, he had to borrow vacation time to make it happen. He was not thrilled about his entire family taking off for a year. He would miss us, and we would miss him immeasurably as well. But he has an open heart and generally accepts his wife's crazy notions.

What made the family separation conceivable for all of us was a trip home at the end of the year to celebrate Christmas and the beginning of the new year together. That made it feel like two semesters instead of a full year. Reliance on the long-familiar academic calendar was somehow comforting for all of us. So that was the plan.

The days and nights just prior to our departure were filled with anxiety for me. Had I packed the anti-malaria medicine for Kenya? Did we have enough socks for our hike in Spain? Had I loaded all the email addresses onto my small netbook computer? When we took our bags to the car, we seemed to have an impossibly small amount of stuff. Would it be enough for four months away, with winter coming on? I fretted, and a part of me was certain that the whole trip was a terrible idea. But then the plane lifted off, and I suddenly let myself feel the adventure of it all. My anxieties drifted away as the trees, buildings and harbors of home got smaller and smaller through the plane window, and suddenly I was filled with a sense of euphoria. This adventure was actually going to happen! I looked at the three children, all of them relaxed and confident, reading their books. Apparently, they had more confidence in their mother than she had in herself. They never doubted that we would pull it off. I considered my traveling companions, and I saw what a gift the Big Trip would be for all of us: a time out of time, a time to learn without the structures and strictures of home. A time to simply *be*, out of a lifetime of doing.

From my journal:

This year is a wonderful gift. When we feel claustrophobic with each other, I remember that I am so lucky to have the children close this year, with no agenda, no school. There is almost limitless free time to enjoy each other, to be together. I hear them joking with each other as they do the dishes after dinner. Evan is giving them a lecture on music, and all three are comparing notes about their favorite TV programs and movies at home. They admire him so much. I can hear beneath the words his gentle assertion of authority, his willingness to share with them the accumulated wisdom of his eighteen years. I smile inside. This is time that they have missed while they were busy in school, but they did experience this togetherness as I had hoped. And what a gift for me to listen in!

Evan bought a guitar here in Guatemala, and he is quite skilled. I hear him playing on the terrace in the evenings. Laura and Conor have learned a lot of Spanish, and they understand almost everything they hear. I so appreciate each of them, even their foibles. Where would Laura be without her indecisiveness? Where would Conor be without his self-assurance? And where would Evan be without his occasional moodiness? I am blessed to have them all in my family.

When I tell people that I am taking my three teens on this trip, they often say, "How courageous!" I love to travel, especially abroad. So I don't see it as courageous. But the root word of courageous is **heart** *and in this way, it truly describes our journey. A journey of love. The opportunity to spend unlimited time with my family, unprogrammed and unrushed. The last time we had this much time together was before Evan started kindergarten.*

Besides spending unprogrammed time together, another motivation for the Big Trip was that I felt the need to unprotect my kids. To take them out of the coddling consumerism that surrounds teenagers in the United States. Where following international news is seen as somehow deviant, and where caring about people on the other side of the world is unusual. To leave the island that is the United States, even temporarily, and immerse them in other ways of living. Some ask, "But couldn't you do that here in this country? There are other cultures right down the street and places where American affluence is as foreign as in much of the developing world." The answer is yes of course we could have done that. But anyone who has cared for teens knows that directing them is like herding cats. Teens are self-directed and not always in directions helpful to them. With teens, total immersion is often the best way to go. Taken out of their home environments, they are forced to live differently. Thrown into new environments, everyone can learn the ropes together, without defensiveness or posturing. Their naturally inquisitive natures take over, and they are open to learning.

Listening and learning were on the list I had before the trip. Listening to what other cultures have to teach us, and learning that our culture does not have all the answers. In fact, we have much to learn as a culture here in the United States, and humility is one of the major items. I hoped that the kids—and I—would come back humbler and better informed.

Our educational focus for the trip was a linguistic one. Anyone who has not been a consumer of public education in the United States in the last decade might not know this, but foreign language instruction has been decimated in our schools. My younger children had attended a charter school, kindergarten through eighth grade, which could afford no foreign language instruction at all. This is not unusual. Many schools are down to a few years only, teaching one or maybe two languages.

I feel strongly that learning a foreign language well enough to communicate is a key part of education. Learning one of the romance languages teaches the linguistic roots of Western thought necessary to understanding many fields from science to poetry. Learning any foreign language helps us to listen closely. It also develops mental flexibility. The moment when we first wrap our minds around the concept that "we just can't translate that directly—we have to find a different expression for it!" is an important one in our lives. Some phrases are so intertwined with the culture they spring from that they can't be disentangled. Language learning helps to develop an open mind, as language, culture, and politics are intertwined.

Knowing the language where one is traveling is like knowing a secret code. We were thrilled to read the billboards and understand the slang on the streets of Spain, some of which we could then practice in our conversations. Overhearing conversations on the street, chatting with store owners, listening to the radio—all of our experiences are so much richer when we can understand what is being said. Speaking the language opens doors to understanding and to our interactions with people. We were able to attend political lectures where we traveled and to learn at a depth that tourists generally do not reach.

So we planned our trip around language immersion. We chose Spanish since all three kids knew the language to some degree, and their mother was more or less proficient in it. It is also a very useful language, the second most commonly spoken language in the world, behind Chinese. One of our main organizing principles for the year was Spanish immersion, with the goal of better Spanish language skills for all of us.

As I think about what I wanted for my kids on the Big Trip, I often forget what I wanted for myself and more important, what I got that I didn't ask for. One of those was the education I received from my kids. Kids are amazing teachers of their parents. My teens shook me out of my complacency when we traveled together. When I was tired, they had unending energy for learning and introspection about what they saw. When I was ready to complain, they reminded me to shed my notions of what I should expect from a situation, to drop my impatience about how things are done elsewhere. I wrote, "No one complains—about muddy shoes, eating food they don't like, being caught in the rain without a rain jacket—all the things that used to bother them." This became a joke in the family, so much so that complaining was strictly forbidden by general agreement.

Once, after riding a bus in Bolivia for thirty hours without the rest and meal stops that accompany long-distance bus trips in the United States, I made a negative comment. I felt tired, dirty and impatient to get off the bus. I thought that I was intuiting their needs, as mothers often try to do. To be completely honest, the complaining was from my own heart, about my own needs. All three kids looked at me reproachfully. "Mom, are we complaining again?"

Of all the family members, I had the hardest time dropping my expectations, my concern to make things right. Perhaps I would have been more accepting had I traveled alone. I was generally the travel director, and as such I was prone to judging, to second-guessing my decisions, and occasionally to complaining, despite my best efforts. The kids taught me that they were able to rise above whatever challenges came our way, to face them with good humor better than their impatient mother.

One day we walked around the suburbs of Madrid for an hour in the rain towing our suitcases, and impossibly, carrying our frame backpacks as well. It was one of few major transitions that we made, because we generally stayed in one place for long stretches. I had the address of a hotel where we had planned to stay the night prior to an early flight to Kenya the following morning. But somehow the reality on the ground didn't match up with the directions we had been given. What was to be a short walk from the subway stop turned into a long march in the cold and rain, through residential and commercial neighborhoods. It was like a bad dream, one where you meet frustration after frustration and never get where you are going. We could not even find a cab driving those deserted residential streets or a pedestrian out on a drizzly afternoon who could point us in the right direction.

Eventually we did make it, with enough time for a good night's sleep before heading out early to the airport. I'd like to say that no one, including me, complained about that long, unhappy walk, or about the fact that once we'd arrived, we discovered that there was no restaurant in the neighborhood and so no dinner. I remember berating myself for my lack of planning. As the mother and tour director, I often took on too much, trying to make everything go well all the time. True to their promises, the kids didn't complain. It was another of many learning experiences for me.

There were lots of other lessons for me, some of which I'm still learning—patience being the biggest one. Waiting for three teens to get up and out the door in the morning reminded me daily of the need for patience. Sometimes I wished for a school schedule to whip them into shape or even another adult to take a turn. Sometimes I left them on their own and rejoiced in the freedom to wander new places on my own schedule. But the enjoyment of being in community with my family members always compensated for the trials, and each day I woke up ready for more.

We spent nearly a year traveling together as a family. It was an incredible gift for each of us, one that we feel so lucky to have experienced. We had saved and planned for several years in order to do this, and in fact the year cost less than our everyday lives at home. We traveled light, bought little, and lived simply. Buying knick-knacks is out of the question when you are living out of a small suitcase. Airfare was the largest item in our budget, and we worked to minimize air travel. Nevertheless, we were able to live without my salary for a year because we are luckier than far more than ninety-nine percent of the world's inhabitants. Quaker writer and activist David Zarembka similarly describes his life in Kenya, where he emigrated from the United States. Though his income is modest, he is considered to have immense resources in comparison with most people in Kenya and a responsibility for helping out the community. Being especially blessed with enough resources to live comfortably, he feels called to give some of his resources away. We felt the same way, and by living abroad we learned this lesson deep in our bones.

By telling our tale we hope that other families will consider taking a journey of exploration that will bring them out of their comfort zone so they can return revitalized, ready to work on growing a better world. If a long trip is impossible, a shorter one may work, or annual trips to the same place. Volunteering opens doors, and there is need for volunteers everywhere. An open heart goes a long way.

Some of our family rules for the year:

Avoid hotels and apartments. Live in community with friends and acquaintances. We relied on our faith community, the Quaker community, which welcomed us in each of the countries where we were based. We made financial contributions to our hosts and shared meals to lessen their burden of hosting an entire family. Hosting visitors at our home is something we love to do, so we already had friends in many parts of the world. We have been members of an internet-based home exchange service (http://www.intervac-homeexchange.com) for many years, and we visited some of our old and new friends from this program on our trip. Some people exchange homes simultaneously, each visiting the other's home at the same time. Other exchanges are not simultaneous, and can be years apart. In this way, we returned visits to some whom we had hosted years ago. We visited other new families and hope to welcome them to our home in the years ahead. The one time we rented an apartment, we did so in a compound where local families were living, providing us the opportunity to live in community there as well.

Learn a foreign language and speak it as often as possible. I was surprised at how easy this was. Kids actually do pick up languages by immersion. The younger ones, age thirteen, learned three years of Spanish during the year, enrolling in Spanish level four upon their return. They even aced the advanced placement test, gaining college placement credits during their first year in high school.

Avoid fast food and limit restaurant food. Become familiar with the local food and how to cook it. Our family has a rule prohibiting fast food when we travel, so this was expected by all. Instead, we practiced eating slow food. Buying mainly local, unprocessed food, eating only what was in season, and learning recipes from our hosts were joyful aspects of the year.

Practice slow travel. Stay in a few places only and move via local transportation. My friend Peg suggested that we stay in only one location for the whole year, but we could not bear to limit ourselves that much. We lived in three countries over the year with side trips to a few others. We stayed in most locations for at least a week and some for two months. We made friends with local shopkeepers and took multiple trips to the same museums, finding new treasures or visiting old favorites again and again.

Make volunteering a part of the fabric of our lives. That is easy. There are ways to help wherever you go. One does not have to be part of an established (often expensive) volunteering abroad program. Many people whom we saw in our travels, even young people alone, had made connections via Skype or email with a non-profit organization and worked directly with people they had met online. Many such organizations are accustomed to accepting visiting volunteers and offer help with housing and getting situated. With some advance research, a good volunteer placement can be set up independently. In our case, I had made contacts with several organizations so that we had a general plan of what we would be doing in each location before we arrived.

Friends have said to me, "I could not conceive of doing this, much as I would like. I have too many responsibilities here at home." To those people, I suggest a shorter travel period if that seems right. What about a short leave of absence from work, volunteering for a month-long stretch in the summer? Airfare is the biggest item. After that it does not have to be a big financial obligation. Due to currency inequalities, the US dollar goes far in much of the global south. It does not have to cost a lot. Further, many parents can continue working while traveling. Many people work remotely now and need only a connected laptop for equipment. Internet connections are becoming more reliable all over the world. Some people have told me that when they were living abroad, their clients did not even notice the difference!

There are many ways to get off the treadmill of modern life for a time. Some have travelled the world with a focus on wildlife, or worked in organic gardening in exchange for room and board. Some have lived on a family boat and joined the international traveling boat community. Others have created a family circus and traveled around the continental US. One couple I know started out traveling for a year and has not been able to quit. They are going on their seventh year, with consulting income and travel blogs supporting their work.

But what about school? I am not a school teacher. I was one of those parents who breathed a sigh of relief when kindergarten started, and the professionals took over formal education of my children. The idea of ordering textbooks and worksheets online for home-schooling makes me break into a cold sweat. So I decided not to teach them, but rather to let them learn on their own. Releasing them from the expectation of advancing a year in school took the pressure off. On their own, they visited museums and wrote papers. On their own, they read, studied Spanish and conversed in Spanish. The younger ones enrolled in an online math program to keep up their skills. My only requirement of them was to write, and they did a lot of that. Much of our writing, theirs and mine, was published on a family blog, at http://www.cuentosdelcamino123.blogspot.com. Some of that writing forms the backbone of this book.

WALKING THE CAMINO DE SANTIAGO

To begin our Big Trip, we decided to ground ourselves by taking a long walk—for three weeks straight. We chose to walk a portion of the Camino de Santiago through northern Spain, a path that has been used since the Middle Ages for pilgrimages to Santiago de Compostela, the city and cathedral which is the final resting place of the Apostle James. Long prior to that, it was a Roman road walked by soldiers maintaining their westernmost outposts. Soldiers left their stone-carved graffiti on the trail, with one sign reading, "Seventh Roman legion was here". The road has been walked by Visigoth conquerors, Moorish invaders, and other more recent soldiers. The famous Chanson de Roland, which I remembered from my high school French class, features a battle between French and Spanish troops on the Camino. The knight who was the inspiration for Don Quixote de la Mancha supposedly fought off one hundred and fifty knights on a Roman bridge here in the fourteenth century. On the Camino, there is a sense of living in a history book.

This *French Way* is actually one of several *caminos*, or walking routes, through Spain. It was given that name by the Spanish because it begins in France, traveling across the Pyrenees to Spain, and then across the north of Spain to Santiago, in the western corner of Galicia. Traces remain of other Camino routes throughout Europe. Some are networks of country paths, while others exist only through oral memory and can be followed by guesswork and a continual process of getting lost and then finding one's way. Some people we met on the Camino had started walking in Paris, others in Germany or even in their own backyards in England. Other routes lead to Santiago as well, including the *Ruta del Plata*, the Silver Road, starting in the south of Spain. We were to experience first-hand the connections between the old world and the new later on when we visited Toledo, Spain and then learned about the origin of its silver in Potosí, Bolivia. But the French route is the most famous route.

People walk the Camino for spiritual, religious, athletic and other reasons. Walkers are generally called "pilgrims," connoting the spiritual nature of the walk for many. As befits a program organized by the Catholic Church, a formal certificate or *compostela* is composed in Latin for those who are able to prove that they have walked at least one hundred kilometers of the distance. The certificate bears a seal and a signature from a special office connected with the Church in Santiago.

Our purpose, like that of many pilgrims, was not particularly religious in the strict sense. We chose to start off our Big Trip with a Camino walk as a way of grounding ourselves, setting time aside from our daily lives and beginning our "slow travel" year. Since we are a Quaker family, we were drawn to the idea of extended contemplation time. It would be an intentional spiritual walk, a time to reflect on our year to come and where we found ourselves in our lives.

The Camino travels through small villages and big cities, with extremely well marked paths. The sign for the Camino is the scallop shell, or in French, the *coquille St. Jacques*. The shell takes its French name from the Apostle James himself, a wonderful example of history and culture embedded in language. The ribs in the shell symbolize the routes people can take to the center point, the Cathedral in Santiago where St. James is said to be interred. The scallop shell is pictured all along the route, so that even walkers who may have stopped at a roadside café and imbibed a bit too much sangria for lunch can easily find the path again. For us, it was wonderful never having to worry about whether we were on the correct path.

The kids pause to reflect on the first day on the Camino

There are various options for lodgings on or near the Camino, including hotels, hostels (called *pensiones*) and *albergues*. Albergues are bunk room establishments set up by government, church or private organizations to serve pilgrims on the Camino. We typically stayed in albergues when we could, as it was the most traditional (often going back centuries) and economical option. Also, that way we met interesting fellow pilgrims from all over the world. Getting to know our fellow travelers was one of the best parts of the Camino. Meals were sometimes provided in the albergues for a small fee, and when they were not provided there was usually a simple kitchen where travelers could cook a meal. We found them to be generally clean and very safe, similar to the AMC (Appalachian Mountain Club) huts in New England. The luxury of hot water showers led to a much better-smelling environment than one often finds when sleeping near through-hikers on the Appalachian Trail!

Conor's backpack – laundry line

We got up every day well before dawn, requiring an adjustment to our usual habits. On the Camino, it was obligatory. Pilgrims are required to clear out by eight o'clock, to allow the cleaning crew to take over for the next day's travelers. Given that Spain shares a time zone with most of Europe, sunrise was generally about eight o'clock in September. As a result, headlamps were universal headgear. Walking along in the pre-dawn fog and being present for the dawning of the new day, were new experiences for me, an inveterate night owl. We generally walked with breaks for meals until three or four in the afternoon, sometimes later if we had visited tourist sites along the way or lingered over a picnic lunch.

Walking the Camino is a mildly athletic event, but not a marathon, unless one chooses to make it so. There were some who sped by us, but many more who meandered along at a relaxed, even meditative, pace. Some read Chaucer or inspirational readings along the way. And though Martin Sheen in the movie *The Way* loses his son to a hiking mishap, and Paul Coelho (in *The Pilgrimage*) experiences spiritual hallucinations on the journey, we found it to be a gentle, reflective way to spend a few weeks in harmony with nature and a way to practice living a simpler lifestyle, at least temporarily.

Reflections from my journal on the Camino:

León: The start of our walk, three hundred kilometers from our intended finish at Santiago. We started walking before dawn and decided to step into the cathedral as the rosy rays of the sun were just lighting up its towers. In a side chapel, mass was underway and we joined the few faithful souls who were present at that early hour. The priest soon noticed the presence of a family with backpacks and asked us to come up front, where he gave us the Pilgrim's Blessing, a lovely prayer similar to the familiar Irish blessing. The parishioners welcomed us with smiles of encouragement. An apt beginning to this walk of cultural understanding.

From the sublime to the ridiculous: The previous day, after we had gotten off the city bus in León and prepared to start our first few steps of the Camino, we put our packs down on a park bench to get situated and take a deep breath before this momentous occasion. When I picked up my pack and turned to begin the walk, I lost my balance and fell into a big bush. A gash on my leg promptly opened up and began to bleed profusely. All three kids laughed at my clumsiness, instead of coming to my aid as I would have hoped. Unhappy thoughts of self-pity and criticism of my children coursed through me as I searched through my pack for my first-aid kit. What a way to start!

Santibañes de Valdiglesias: *A small unassuming church-owned albergue turned out to be a morsel of heaven. Our Italian host, Hercules, provided us a meal of roast chicken, risotto and salad at a long table, seating over 20 travelers, in the orchard behind the house. The green leaves above, our festive laundry hanging off to the side, and a friendly hedgehog wandering around under the table completed the scene. Talk ranged from Spanish to French to German to English and from international travel to political affairs. A Korean friend said she had come on the walk in search of diamonds. I was not sure I understood her well, since she spoke with Korean-accented French. I thought maybe she was being poetic, and perhaps she was. Then I learned that she was single and unattached. In a larger sense, I suppose we are all here looking for diamonds of various sorts.*

Near Hospital de Orbigo: *After hours of walking along a quiet plateau with no villages of any sort, we came on an old barn with a man sitting outside, reading a book of spiritual inspiration. In front of him, like a mirage in the desert, was a stand with all sorts of refreshments. Hot tea and coffee, cool juice, nuts and fruits had been laid out with love and care. There was a sign offering us to help ourselves and to make a donation if we wished. This man lives in the barn year-round, offering these gifts as his life's work. The free offering made me wonder how often I am able to make a gift without expecting anything in return. I remembered a sign we have seen on the Camino, "The tourist requires; the pilgrim gives thanks."*

Camino Story by Conor

The phone rang on three lines at the same time, and his Bluetooth provided a constant drone. He swiveled from computer to computer working on anything and everything. He could barely hear the beep of the email saying he had new messages because the computers were working just as hard as he was and putting out a lot of noise. Though this wasn't a bad year financially, he found himself working harder than he had used to, without seeing any change in the mountains of work that appeared everywhere he looked. Time was moving too fast, the deadlines running full speed instead of creeping closer. He couldn't seem to find enough time in his workday, so he always brought work home. He missed countless family events: his daughter's amusement park birthday, his son's championship game, his wife's art show. His family was falling apart while all he thought about were the financial reports for next year.

Bleep! Another email. For the last two weeks since his wife signed him up for a relationship health forum, he has received spam mail nonstop. He usually just glances at them and then puts them in the trash folder, but this one caught his eye at its sheer ridiculousness. The Camino de Santiago was a path across most of Spain, starting at different spots in Europe and converging to make one path in France at the Pyrenees. It ended in Santiago, where the bones of Saint James are buried. People just dropped everything and walked the 700 kilometers, living simply and healthily. "What a crazy idea!" he thought. He'd liked hiking as a kid, but as he got older and more mature he had lost interest in wandering around on trails. He just knew his wife would hound him about doing this; she would say how good it would be to get back to his childhood, and nonsense like that.

He finally read more about it and reluctantly prepared to go. He had decided, or rather his wife had decided, that he would go, and start in St. Jean Pied-de-Port, near the French border. At first he was vehemently opposed to the idea, but he gradually changed his mind. He thought of what kind of a father he'd been, always working. He thought of his 60-hour work week, most of it self-imposed, and made up his mind. He bought all new hiking stuff, quick dry shirts and lightweight sleeping bags. He flew into France, and spent a night in a hotel before starting.

The next day, he got up early and started walking. The sun wasn't up yet, so he used his ultra-Brite LiteTek headlamp. The light reflected off his state of the art hiking boots, brand new, with aeration spots and gel pad cushions, "engineered for a premium walking experience". He didn't want to exhaust himself on the first day, but he had to get over the Pyrenees to keep up with his schedule. His first day went by rather uneventfully, and he thought to spend the night in a small town, halfway down on his descent. He had planned to sleep in hotels or hostels for their privacy, instead of sleeping in a large room full of bunk beds, with a number of strangers as happens in an albergue, or inn.

He arrived in the town and realized that it only had an albergue, and no other places to sleep. He wanted to press on to find a more comfortable bed, but he was starting to get blisters, and knew that blisters can make everything extremely unpleasant. He settled on a private room in the albergue. He checked in, dropped his backpack in the room, and left for dinner.

He had forgotten to lock the door, and realized this half way through his meal, in a restaurant on the other side of the village. As he ate, he thought of all the "thieves" he had seen coming in, and how expensive his things were. He hurried to finish his meal, and left without leaving a tip. He got back to the albergue, saw the door to his room open, and he moved more quickly towards his room. He flung open the door, seeing his pack wasn't on the bed where he had left it. As he surveyed his room, he noticed there was a man sitting next to his backpack, seeming perfectly peaceful and in place. Giving him a quizzical look, the man replied, "There were two teenagers rummaging through your stuff, but I scared them away, and made sure no one took anything." He tried to offer him money for his act of kindness, but the man said "No, I won't take your money. Just think of this as a favor to pass on to someone else, and you'll truly experience the Camino de Santiago".

A Camino Poem by Laura

Soft rolling words
Remind me of Spanish hills -
How they rise slowly
Then fall,
Sending you tumbling
Over bumpy "r" s
And smooth, double "l" s.

In this garden,
We let our voices drop,
Like we're in a cathedral.
Maybe there is something sacred
In the silence.

From my journal:

Cruz de Ferro: *An iron cross at the top of the mountain at the highest point of the Camino, where travelers place a stone of remembrance or intention. The pile of stones is many meters high, a visible sign of the vast numbers who have passed this way before us. I placed a stone in memory of my father and a note reading: "For all our ancestors" with a Lakota song in my heart. My father would have liked it here.*

Rabanál del Camino: *The absolute silence of the trail is astonishing. No motors anywhere. By mutual agreement, we walk in silence for at least an hour each day, with the space between us often stretching to over a kilometer. After jokes, discussions and arguments in the morning, everyone is ready for some quiet time almost every afternoon. Quiet country lanes with high hedgerows, streams, yellow fields just harvested, and green trees overarching the path. My thoughts slow down to a meditative speed; the rhythm of my walking is soothing. How natural is this rhythm! For so many years people have walked wherever they were going, thinking their thoughts or observing nature without the constant presence of iPods distracting them from simply living in the present moment.*

Somewhat like the slow food experience, this is the slow travel experience. I taste the sweetness of each blackberry, see the texture of each flower and notice the single stray poppy rising up from a field of recently harvested grain. I note the precise shape of each sharp stone under my foot, the smell of the cow droppings, and the roar of the trucks when the path takes us close to highways. I taste ripe grapes from a vineyard, reminding me that the Romans brought the cultivation of grapes for wine here. We all agree that we have never tasted a better grape.

Cathedral ceiling at Burgos

A wild passion flower in bloom

Walking starts to feel like a natural pace. Hurrying seems abnormal. I can hardly relate to my memories of home, where I would never walk three miles to the grocery store or even one-half mile to the pharmacy. The kids fall easily into the same rhythm as well, with no complaints.

It is astonishing how wild the Camino feels, how unspoiled the landscape. Occasionally we traverse city streets where we are reminded of what century we live in, but this happens much more seldom than I had anticipated. City planners have taken into account the path of the Camino over the centuries, allowing for a cordon of open space surrounding the trail wherever possible. Only occasionally do we walk along breathing engine fumes.

I am aware of the people who have walked this road before me, the incredible depth of the known history of this path. My own cultural heritage comes to me, with the sight of the ever-present magpies in the fields. I am accompanied by the English song "The Magpie" by David Dodds, using the words to an old rhyme about the bird whose calls were thought to tell the future:

One's for sorrow, two's for joy
Three's for a girl and four's for a boy
Five's for silver, six for gold,
Seven for a secret never told
Devil, devil, I defy thee; devil, devil, I defy thee

In my cultural background there is a history of living close to nature, simple lives mixing pantheism with an earlier Christian faith, and a yearning to know the future.

Thank you, Fernando, the hospidalero *(host) at the albergue in Rabanál, who patiently treated Laura's blisters. When we started out on our way the next morning, the stars above the garden were bright and beautiful.*

Trabadela: *Long skirts, bells, rosaries, crosses and underarm odor come to me as thought-memories of years gone by along the trail. I tried omitting deodorant while on the Camino for historical authenticity but my family protested.*

John and Evan pass through a typical village, Galicia

We are learning about other branches of Christianity that have since died out. In the old days, thieves often accosted pilgrims on the Camino, and a group of radical Christians called the Knights Templar protected them. The Knights Templar pioneered the use of the line of credit, accepting letters attesting to pilgrims' assets at home as a guarantee of payment. The knights were known as honest and trustworthy, though not non-violent. In the fourteenth century, the last of them were executed by the Catholic authorities, but many of their round temples and other buildings remain, echoes of branches of Christian thought that no longer exist.

We pass elderly farmers in Galicia harvesting potatoes with two-pronged wooden pitchforks and wooden plows. There is a fine line between quaintness and grinding poverty—no line at all for those living that life, I imagine. Many homes in the area are abandoned. Though some are coming back from the brink, some are headed downhill, and some entire villages have been given up entirely.

O'Cebreiro: *After a nine hundred meter climb to the top of the ridge we arrived at this little town, the gateway to Galicia. We decided that the long hike is useful for pilgrims, because it takes that long to learn to pronounce the town's name. All five syllables, with the "th" for the "C" as is proper in Castellano, the Spanish of much of Spain. Though the language in the area is actually Gallego, the Castillian soft "C" is still used here. We finally got it pretty much straight, in just enough time to feel the cold fog at the top and sit down to a wonderful meal of* caldo gallego—*vegetable soup. My vegetable-starved body is in heaven. Two weeks of dry cheese and ham on white bread is getting old.*

The story I liked best in O'Cebreiro: the parishioner travels in the cold snow to the church, where the grumbling parish priest has to open up the church to offer mass to him. The wine turns to Christ's blood, a miracle honoring the steadfastness of the worshiper's faith. When I went into that quiet ancient church and felt the prayers of so many generations, I could sense a bit of that faith that could perform miracles.

Fonfría: *The name means "village of the cold fountain". Its water may be cold but its heart is warm. The albergue is run by Pedro, a Cuban expatriate, who operates a beautiful hostel along a cool mountain ridge.*

He offers us a communal meal of hot stew, followed by board games, and a stay in a renovated palloza, *an ancient round hut used by the Galicians. Clean as a whistle and lots of fun, with dancing and Cuban music warming the cockles of our hearts.*

Sárria: A town famous for its location, 100 kilometers from the end of the Camino in Santiago. Travelers must start from here on foot, and no closer, in order to receive the Compostela, *the certificate of completion that guarantees a pilgrim a spot in heaven. The catch is, you must not sin again. Lucky are the few who expire upon arriving at Santiago. The names of the less lucky ones who did not make it are marked with crosses by the side of the trail.*

100 kilometers to go: sign and shrine

As a result of this status, Sárria is crowded. Lots of people take the train up from Madrid on weekends to walk the last 100 kilometers. The presence of iPods and fresh city clothes increases dramatically. For the first time, we had to scramble to find a place to stay. We were lucky to find rooms in a hostel, where we shared dinner with three retired Frenchmen who had walked together since Limoges, France. They were celebrating their sixtieth day on the Camino. One of them said, "When you arrive in Santiago, you will feel no pain at all! Any blisters or soreness will disappear immediately when you hug the statue of Saint James!" I admired their faith and wondered whether I could ever believe in the Catholic saints as they do.

People walking the Camino speak of "my Camino", as in: "I have been planning my Camino for years." There is a desire for a very deep experience, one that will change one's life, and many people say the Camino has changed their lives. As for us, whether our Camino changed our lives remains to be seen.

I decided that we should call "our" Camino the "Sendero de las Moras", or Blackberry Path. The blackberries have ripened along with our elevation gain, as the days go on and as we have traveled to the higher and cooler areas of Galicia. We seem to reach each region just as its blackberries reach their peak of ripeness, purple and juicy. All the hedgerows are full of berries, providing a tasty snack as we go along.

We have seen many inspirational quotes and travelers' graffiti, which I find a welcome mental distraction: "Ánimo!" in the hard spots, or "Keep it up!" "Ke keda poco!" towards the end , or "Not much left!" (in internet-style streamlined Spanish). And my favorite, carved into the exterior wall of a church leaving Astorga early on, a word puzzle that goes like this:

GUÍA SEÑOR MI CAMINO
SEÑOR MI CAMINO GUÍA
MI CAMINO GUÍA SEÑOR
CAMINO GUIA SEÑOR MI

"Guide my path, O Lord". Visually arresting as a verbal puzzle, it is a phrase that has stayed with me and guides my steps. I am lucky to be one who is able to look past religious differences to use a phrase in my meditation that some might find objectionable because of disagreements with its language. This phrase reminds me to let my steps be guided by Spirit. I am not the one who is in charge, but that holy power that I can't put into words, that power that I am aware of in my best moments. It

is good to practice this phrase when difficulties crop up with my fellow travelers, my children. Traveling with family has challenges that the solitary traveler avoids. We have an opportunity to put our learning to work right away with our loved ones.

Arzúa: *So many different travelers: Maria from Valencia, who talks with and welcomes everyone into her circle; Michael, who walked from Frankfurt, Germany and is a kindred spirit; Sander, a teenager from Holland traveling alone, who accompanied us for several days and kept us all happy with his jokes. All have something to teach us.*

Again, there are gifts on the road. Someone has made some fresh raspberry marmalade and roasted chestnuts. Both are offered in little individual cups, with a small sign asking for donations to support the work.

Santiago and Salamanca: *The day was bookended with the full moon to begin and end it. We started walking under the moon's light in the early morning and walked into Santiago, the end of the Camino. We arrived in time to obtain our Compostelas and attend the noontime mass. Then we picked up our rental car, an infrequent luxury, and drove from Santiago to Salamanca. We arrived late at night, in time to see the full moon shining on the yellow stones of Salamanca's Plaza Major, or main square. We are rocked in the embrace of the moon, remembering the Camino in our dreams.*

SLOW TRAVEL IN SPAIN AND FRANCE

We spent the rest of the fall moseying around Spain and southern France, with a side trip to Morocco and one to Kenya. Our itinerary was anchored by stays with friends and by vacation spots we were offered through the Intervac home exchange program. For many years, we have hosted travelers from this program at our home, not knowing whether these little IOUs would ever come in handy. Intervac, the world's oldest home exchange program, is a network of households worldwide who have offered to host another family and then in turn be hosted by someone else. Sometimes the stays are simultaneous, but often they are not. We often "paid it forward" in this way. On our Big Trip the tables were turned. Several families in Spain and Argentina hosted us graciously, many of them becoming new friends. Perhaps one day we will be able to return the favor by hosting them.

One wonderful family offered us their apartment in Madrid for three weeks, allowing us to immerse ourselves in the Spanish culture and language, getting to know our neighbors and visiting the Prado Museum every day. There we undertook the most studious part of our year, as we delved into research projects supplemented by intensive reading and museum trips. The younger two were assigned to write a long research paper, lest at age thirteen they forget how to read and write. I could have benefited from the same, but my older son and I chose to spend the time reading and exploring the wonders of Madrid.

I tend to be quite brazen when it comes to travel opportunities. Once at a Quaker conference a few years prior to the Big Trip, I met Rebecca who lives south of Toulouse. Having grown up in New York State, she now lives within a day's drive of the mysterious cave paintings and other treasures of the Lot Valley and the Dordogne region of France. "May I have your address?" I asked her. "I might travel there someday soon and would love to visit you!" Lucky for us, she loves to have visitors from the States. Rebecca put us up for a few nights and even helped us plan some visits to hidden places we never would have discovered without her. When we visited a castle further north that she had suggested, she passed us along to her friend Karina, who hosted us for a night and show us around her village. All these people are now good friends of my family, and they are welcome in our home at any time.

Barcelona is the home of our dear friends Nuria and Pep, another family whom we had met on the internet home exchange program. Our first connection occurred several years earlier through our older sons, both of whom were looking for a way to exchange language and travel. The sense of trust that is created between families who share their children is quite amazing. First, Victor came to stay with us when he turned 16, and we were able to show him New England. Then his family came for a visit, and we had a memorable summer holiday together. Among other wonderful memories was the day we all gathered in our kitchen as they taught us how to make simple Spanish *pan con tomate* after a Saturday at the beach. Then it was our turn to visit them in Barcelona. We used their home as a base to explore the city, and had some incredible adventures together there as well.

Playing hacky sack in Barcelona

There is something melancholy and quite lovely about staying in a beach home after the summer is over. We got to know the beaches south of Valencia and Granada in this way, staying in condominiums on the coast, again offered by our Intervac friends. South of Granada we stayed near Segovia's last home, imagining his guitar playing as we sat on the beach. We listened to the autumn wind blowing through the windows, and swam in the still-warm Mediterranean.

LOT VALLEY:

When we pulled up to Karina's home, there was a grape harvest underway. Men in rubber boots were hauling hoses around, and the tiny village was completely absorbed in its work. Karina's daughter, Gen, and our kids hung out in the quiet garden while Karina and I prepared dinner together in the kitchen. In the Pêche Merle *caves, the creations of the long-ago cave artists could be hanging in a modern art museum today. Horses galloping, with the horse's haunch formed from a rounded rock protrusion. Arrows flying. You can almost hear the hoof beats. The Castle of Cenevière has been owned by the same family since the Middle Ages. There are personal letters from King Charles I of Spain and a wall of frescoes with views of the owner's trip to the East on the Crusades.*

Karina's welcoming kitchen in the Lot Valley

Conor's reflection on the life of a 14th century monk in Queribus Castle, Cucugnon, France

December 8th, 1342

The harsh wind woke me up this morning, along with the steeple bell, just as dawn was beginning to break. I would have frozen to death had it not been for the fire smoldering in the corner, which licked at the wall as I went to sleep last night. I got off my small hard bed and walked to the well, full of water from yesterday's rain. I made my way into the dining hall and sat down on the long bench. There were bowls of steaming hearty soup on the table, next to tough bread. Other monks filed in behind me and sat down on the bench. We ate in silence, as Brother Martin read us passages from the Holy Book. I enjoyed every warming drop of that soup and prepared myself to make the trek down the mountain, into the town below. We were out of vegetables, and we couldn't grow them in our monastery because of the harsh weather most of the year. Once I had finished, I got my cloak and left the castle.

A modern-day monk at the abandoned Queribus Castle

The wind rustled in the trees, and it sounded like whispers. The sun was up, although it wasn't warming me at all. I wrapped my cloak around me more tightly and enjoyed the brief feeling of warmth that it brought. At the bottom of the hill, I looked at the distance I had just descended and realized I would need to go back up, burdened by my purchases. On the way to the market, I walked along the cobblestone street and glanced at all the small houses with thatched roofs. Their doors were shut tight to ward off the biting chill that had a way of sneaking through cracks.

I arrived at the center square, sheltered from the wind by the towering church. The market was open, although the only stands were shivering in the corner. I walked over and looked over the measly leftovers of the harvest. I picked out all the vegetables that weren't noticeably infested with bugs, which amounted to just enough. I walked back up the mountain and brought the vegetables into the kitchen. I sat down to work on copying scripts, and the day melted fast, as it usually does when I become enchanted in my work. Dinner was more soup, which I enjoyed, tasting the vegetables that were the result of my labors. I fell asleep next to the fire, absorbing its caring warmth.

BARCELONA:

Over the last weeks we have settled down to a good travel pace, with time visiting friends and time by ourselves to absorb what we've learned and of course to keep up our Spanish practice. When I drive long distances, we usually have a Spanish lesson for Laura and Conor. "Mom, let's go over the future tense." Giving Spanish lessons while driving is particularly helpful in taking my mind off the anxiety I feel driving narrow mountain roads. It is amazing how conjugating verbs in Spanish makes me forget the very real possibility of going over the cliff. Someone should do a study on this as a method of eliminating fear of heights.

They are learning the tenses and vocabulary pretty quickly, and our verb book is our constant companion. I am really pleased at how interested they are to learn Spanish and understand what our hosts are saying. They remember a phrase they didn't understand and ask me hours later to explain it. I wish I had a memory like that!

We spent last week in Barcelona with our friends Nuria and Pep and their three children. Though they speak Catalán at home, they were kind enough to limit themselves to Castilian Spanish with us so that we were not totally at sea. They had a long weekend off work and were able to take time to tour around with us. Last weekend Spain celebrated the Fiesta de la Hispanidad, *or celebration of Hispanic unity, which was interesting to observe in Cataluña, with its strong regional identity and some separatist tendencies. Though the celebration is marked by military parades in other parts of Spain, there was very little of that in Cataluña. We did see some motorcyclists waving an oversized Spanish flag at one intersection. Other than that, it was a typical long weekend for Barcelonans, with tapas, strolling on the Ramblas, and hanging out at museums. At least that's what we did. The MNAC, the Spanish abbreviation for the Cataluñan National Art Museum, has the most incredible collection of Romanesque frescoes anywhere in the world. They have been removed from various churches throughout the province in order to protect them. There must be forty different church naves in the museum, and they are gorgeous.*

Although delving into the art of twelfth-century churches was fascinating, the most interesting aspect of Barcelona for me was the Gaudí architecture. Gaudí's work seems so outlandish that it's hard to fit it into nineteenth century European notions. It came out of the Catalán Modernismo *movement, related to Art Nouveau, but it seems even more colorful and playful than most Art Nouveau I have seen. It looks like Matisse gone three-dimensional, with his Mediterranean colors and fantastical shapes. There are twenty-foot lizards and rooflines that drip as if they are melting. One of my favorite Gaudí works is the Park Guell, where he designed an entire neighborhood. It was never finished, but was to include housing, parks, and other community spaces. Among the completed portions are a residence (a pink house complete with steeple) and a large park which overlooks Barcelona. It has wonderful curving benches, decorated with pieces of ceramic tiles and old bottles. People flock to the Park Guell, not just tourists but Barcelona residents. It is quirky, fun and very Mediterranean.*

Touring Barcelona with Nuria and Pep was a joy

Gaudí's largest and last work is the design of a new modern cathedral, the Sagrada Familia. In the last decade of his life, he applied his gift for modern interpretation of traditional spaces to a huge cathedral, complete with many huge spires, statues with Biblical stories and a tremendous nave. Though he died in 1926, the work on the project continues today; cranes and construction workshops fill the church.

Barcelonans are helping to pay for the construction of this huge community project. Though I found the oversized Biblical figures a bit gaudy (as it were), the idea of building a new cathedral for modern times is a very striking one.

Tarragona Roman Chariot Races—*(a historical vignette) See how the chariots burst out of the tunnel and around the corner! Who will be first? Will I win my bet? One horse is bloodied—it must have grazed the side of the tunnel as it rushed along. The tunnel is barely wide enough for one chariot pulled by a team of four horses. Overtaking might well lead to injury, or even death for a horse or rider. Standing with my family in the amphitheater, I am enveloped in a summer haze, amplified by the spectators and the dust thrown up by the winning chariot as he takes a victory lap around the stadium.*

Evan's rules for the Big Trip were different from those for his younger siblings. At eighteen, he could have planned his own gap year. He came and went as he wanted, though I was pleased that he usually stayed with the family, and went along with most of our tours and volunteering. He was not required to do any writing, and though he did write his own thoughts privately, he shared little. So I was incredibly moved when he shared this song with me about our time in Spain.

Sea-Shells, a song by Evan:

We would wake, to rented beds and dark mornings
We would take our cheese and bread and start walking

And the clouds would sink beneath us,
As we changed sunscreen for our sweaters.
And no blisters could defeat us,
Nor could stormy mountain weather.
As our shadows took the trail
Through morning's misty veil,
We grew together.

Sea-Shells
You're our mother, you're our partner, you're our overhanging tree;
Sea-Shells
You led us to Santiago, now you've brought us to the sea.

Valencia caught autumn's breeze
But the sand and waves stayed warm.
From five flights up we watched the sea
And heard the breakers form.
As the light drained from the Spanish sky,
We took the breakers by surprise.
And to the sea, returned.

Sea-Shells
You're our mother, you're our partner, you're our overhanging tree;
Sea-Shells
You led us to Santiago, now you've brought us to the sea.

Yes, it's corny, but how sweet is that? I am so lucky to have children who show me that they love me.

VALENCIA:

Valencia seems to suffer from a public relations problem. It is not highlighted on the tourist circuit. In fact, Rick Steves, our generally accurate guide to Spain, didn't bother to visit it and left Valencia out of his book. However, it is a completely gorgeous jewel of a city, of a walkable size, with surprises around every corner in the shape of well-restored seventeenth century apartment buildings, Roman and Visigoth ruins, an exciting modern art museum and a beautiful Mercado Central, *or central market. Even the traffic works, due to recent road design work.*

By the way, it also has the Holy Grail. Remember the chalice that Jesus used at the Last Supper, which everyone has been looking for, from Monty Python to Dan Brown? Well we can stop looking. It's in the Cathedral in Valencia, sitting in a little side chapel, in a glass case, all by itself.

It is completely intact. Good thing no one broke it, or we would have tiny shards of the Holy Grail in churches all over Europe. It was in the private possession of various royals until 1506 or thereabouts, when King Alphonsus I gave it to the City of Valencia. Or perhaps, according to an alternative history, Alphonsus put the chalice in hock to borrow money from the church, and it became the property of the church when he could not repay the funds.

We have visited the beach every day for a swim in the Mediterranean. But Valencians consider it wintertime and so they are done with going to the beach. It reminded me of many beach communities I've visited in early fall: golden days, warm water, and a feeling of melancholy after everyone has left for the season.

An old friend of mine from Germany joined us in our exploration of Valencia. Iris and I wandered the streets, exploring all the little squares and side streets. With the kids, we visited the new aquarium, which must be one of the best in the world. It has a number of separate buildings, each dedicated to a different part of the world, from the Red Sea to the Arctic. Sharks, sea horses, and even a Baby Beluga may be seen up close and personal.

I'm putting Valencia on my list of favorite cities in the world.

GRANADA:

This week we switched gears—many times, actually—and drove down to Granada where we visited the Alhambra. It is the greatest Moorish palace in existence, built in the 1300s before Isabel and Ferdinand (dubbed by the Pope "the Catholic Monarchs") drove out the Moors from southern Spain. The year 1492 was big on this side of the Atlantic as well as ours. It was the year that the Moorish regime was finally expelled from Granada, its last redoubt in Spain. In fact, the Hall of the Ambassadors at the Alhambra was the location where Columbus met with the Catholic Monarchs and got his traveling papers, as well as where Boabdil, the last Moorish king (Abu Abdullah in Arabic, otherwise known as Boabdil the Unlucky) agreed to leave this exquisite palace and head south.

The Alhambra: Patio de los Arrayanes

The most famous story about Boabdil may not be true. It is said that as he left Granada, he took one look back at the city and wept. His mother made this rather shrewish remark, "Do not weep like a woman for what you did not know how to defend as a man." Though the remark may not be true, Boabdil's shield from 1492 is still in existence, in the Royal Museum in Madrid. Seeing the actual shield gave me the goose bumps.

I had expected to be impressed by the Alhambra, but its beauty took our breath away. Despite a good deal of ham-handed renovation over the centuries, it is clear that the original designers of the palace were extremely gifted in mathematics, hydraulics, and in creating very beautiful spaces to glorify Allah. Fountains, pools and flowing streams are everywhere. The walls are decorated with three-dimensional tessellations, or repeating geometric shapes. They inspired the artist M.C. Escher in his drawings that use positive and negative spaces to create optical illusions. Recent study has shown that the gardens and buildings were designed using the Pythagorean Theorem, which creates a feeling of natural order and harmony. I guess the Moors really did invent modern mathematics.

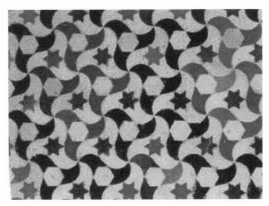

Tessalation pattern at the Alhambra

The Fountain of the Lions is an incredible structural element. Twelve stone lions stand in a circle and support a round pool of water, and through an elaborate mechanism (which was broken during the Spanish conquest and hasn't worked since), the water was to have poured out of their mouths according to the hour of the day. Can you imagine hearing the sound of one lion, two, or twelve, to indicate the time? The lions are undergoing cleaning and restoration, so the fountain had been disassembled at the time of our visit. In their temporary exhibit, we could actually see them much better than had the fountain been assembled. The lions were cut out of marble in such a way that the colored lines in the marble outline the flanks of each. The work is remarkable.

Spain was a Muslim country for 700 years, and much of our "western" culture came from this Moorish influence. The Spanish language retains a lot of Arabic words. European mathematicians learned algebra (as well as the word itself) and the concept of zero from the Moors. In architecture, there was much borrowing back and forth between the cultures. The horseshoe-shaped Visigothic arch (sixth century) and the eleventh-century Romanesque arch were used by the builders of the Alhambra, and the design of Catholic cloisters all over western Europe was based on Moorish palaces and villas.

In Granada we see preserved the beauty as well as the collision of the two cultures. The Spaniards were impressed by the Alhambra, and amazingly did not destroy it completely when they took over. As a result, the languid pools are still full of fish, ancient arches rise over the quiet patios and terraces, and the "fountains of the Water Palace" still flow with cool water. As to the people who created these wonders, they were oppressed, forced to convert to Christianity, and killed if their conversion did not seem genuine. The remaining Moors were expelled to Morocco where they swelled the size of cities such as Fez.

"Granada is the product of two rivers of blood and two cultures in a living encounter." This is a statement by Jose Val del Omar, a Spanish photographer who has produced a film project being shown in the Reina Sophia Museum in Madrid. It is an impressionistic piece with water flowing, children laughing and fish swimming. It feels like a dream. The same could be said of Spain as a whole. Much of Spanish culture came from this encounter, this mixture of East and West.

CÓRDOBA:

The Mezquita – Even more so than the Alhambra, the Mezquita, or mosque, in Córdoba is a harmonious marriage of Moorish and Catholic culture. Moorish civilization — in fact, Islamic cultural development — is said to have reached its acme in Córdoba, home to scientists, mathematicians, and philosophers during the tenth through the fifteenth centuries. The production of paper was brought to Europe here, as was algebra, astronomy and astrology. Christopher Columbus consulted with Moorish scientific advisors before starting on his trip to the "Indies." Interfaith conversations appear to have been beyond tolerant, even collaborative.

The Moors who built the Mezquita in the tenth century respected and preserved the antique Christian Visigothic Church underneath. Instead of erasing the past, they preserved it; remnants can be seen today in the sculptures inside the mosque. After the Reconquista of Spain by Christians, an entire cathedral was built in the center of the Mezquita. Surprisingly, the Christians did not destroy those old walls either. The forest of red and white sandstone columns built by the Moors is still the main event at the Mezquita. Like an ancient forest, the Mezquita allows us to feel surrounded by the divine, so different from the sense of vertical grandeur pulling us heavenward that characterizes Catholic cathedrals.

Around the edge of the building is a series of Catholic chapels which lean into the Mezquita as friends lean on each other. The entire building is a wonderful melding of Christian and Islamic, of different faiths interwoven through time.

The Mezquita in Cordoba, interfaith harmony

Jewish synagogue with Muslim designs, Cordoba

Nearby, in the Jewish quarter of Córdoba, is a small synagogue with Muslim calligraphy on its walls, another reminder of the many cultures that made their home here. The synagogue adds to the understanding of Córdoba as the very center of Moorish civilization in its day, a tolerant community that welcomed scientists and worshipers from throughout the known world.

And She Dreams of Crazy by Laura

Those mountains!
If I were a crazy painter,
I'd pull over to the side of the road and paint for them.
If I were a crazy poet
I'd cut off traffic and drench my page in words for them.
If I were a crazy musician,
I'd play to the core of the world—
No—through the core of the world and back out the other side just for them.

For you,
Mountains.
You with your heartbreaking orange sunset rocks
And deep sea shadows.
You who make me think I could jump
Just jump
Off one of your jagged edges
 And end up flying.

And maybe I could
(For a moment or two)
If I were a crazy painter
Poet
Or musician.
Too bad I'm not crazy
Or a musician, poet, painter, either.
Too bad.
But it wouldn't matter anyways.
I'm not driving.

MADRID:

Attending a lecture: *We spent three solid hours of listening hard, trying to understand the scientists' university lecture on engineering in the developing world. Sometimes I repeat the words silently, letting them roll around in my mouth, hoping that their hard shells will give way to reveal the soft sweetness of understanding within. The Spanish words are like flamenco singing, strong consonants like castanets, alternating with guttural soft "g"s where you do not expect them. Sometimes the speech goes too fast to hold onto a single word, and my mind skims over the cold hard shells. They escape my grasp, and I cannot crack them open. Tired, I let them slide by.*

Signs: *English-language signs are in fashion, lending a sense of the latest style to the goods on offer. We English speakers snicker at the way that foreigners put words together. Instead of "Dunkin' Donuts", there is a coffee shop here called "Dunkin' Coffee". What is being dunked? A nearby cafeteria is called "Flunch", adding a zesty "f" to* the word "lunch". Doesn't it make you want to try the food? I love the name of one store: "So ¡Happy!". It reminds Spaniards that in English the "h" is not silent. When we're done snickering, we go back to trying to understand the fluent Spanish all around us. When you trip over verb tenses and can't find basic vocabulary words, it's hard not to feel stupid!

Thanksgiving: *It is of course a day like any other here. We decided to move it to the weekend so that our hosts could join us in a meal. We looked high and low for cranberries without success. We did find a turkey, chestnuts and wonderful ice creams.* **Calabaza,** *or squash, will substitute for pumpkin, though we did hear that the large orange variety we call pumpkins are sometimes available. We'll be making stuffing by hand, which will do us good. And apple pie can be made everywhere.*

Weather: *Yesterday was the first frost. It came almost a month later than at home, where we usually can count on a frost by Halloween. I went for my morning run and the grass was crispy and white. We do not have our winter coats, so each daily drop in the temperature is greeted by a vague sense of foreboding. The old prehistoric fears work their way in between the cracks in our thinking: What are we doing here, and will we be warm enough come winter? Where is home, and why are we not there? Not wanting to carry extra clothes with us to temperate Kenya next week, we tough it out with sweaters and the old standby, layering. I tell the kids that it doesn't matter what we wear here. They can let go their teenage fashion preoccupations. Shirts under shirts and socks over socks—who cares? They resist, but eventually agree that comfort trumps fashion this year. Many days we wear most of our clothes.*

Walking down a fashionable street in Madrid, my two teens were arguing loudly, and Conor actually pushed Laura into a streetlight. Do other people's teenagers act so badly? I was tired of reminding them to behave respectfully towards each other. Instead, I pulled out my camera and asked them to pose so I could take a picture of them with one of Madrid's signature buildings in the background. They struck a pose, pretending that they were sharing a memorable moment of sibling togetherness.

Striking a pose in Madrid

The Spanish functionary: *We have seen some striking government inefficiency in Spain. The Prado is free from six to eight every night. So at six, there is a long line to the ticket office, where people must go to pick up their free ticket. Then, they must walk clear around the museum to the other door where, after waiting on another long line, they are allowed in. Though it might be more efficient to do away with the ticket altogether* *and have one person with a counter at the door, this would eliminate any number of jobs.*

The post office is something out of Kafka. When you arrive, you take a ticket depending on what you want to do: pick up a package, send a package, or buy an envelope to send something. I arrived with two pieces of business in mind and was already stumped, not knowing which ticket to pick up. After taking a ticket, you wait anywhere from twenty to forty minutes for your number to come up. When you arrive at the window, there is no rush at all to do your business. I had a friendly post office clerk help me to send a package to Morocco. He confided in me that though it would be easier to use a postal meter, he is required to use a certain number of stamps a day, and if he does not, he must buy them personally. So he decorated my package himself. There was no sponge for wetting down those stamps, nor was there a tape dispenser. He had to use his tongue and teeth a lot! When he finished, the entire package was decorated in stamps.

Flamenco: *It is Spanish to the core. It is a mix of Moorish music in the minor key, red and black colors, dramatic moods reflecting Spains's bloody history, and gypsy mystery, from the Roma people who brought it from India many centuries ago. Many of the songs voice the same familiar laments as cowboy tunes, the words just as cheesy. But still they give me goose bumps. A people (or peoples, since flamenco was born in the Romani/ Jewish ghettoes of Spain) oppressed, singing about the tragedy and injustice of life. The songs give voice to the deepest sadness in the world.*

What I see in the marvelous dancing is pride, a regal bearing. The woman tosses her scarf over her shoulder and gives the man a haughty look. The insistent tap dancing moves call attention to the strength and pride of the dancers. Yet the people who created this music lived in caves in Granada, in the Sacramonte (sacred mountain) hills, where they worked as potters and rag sellers. Metalworking was the most elevated profession, one to which many aspired. Even today the residential cave community carries on in Granada, a strong community with deep musical and cultural roots. The place to go for the best flamenco is a warehouse in the urban Roma ghetto outside Seville, the Poligono Sur. *Flamenco today is mixed with drugs and violence, yet flamenco dancers have an incredible mystique. To be a flamenco star is to be a hero in Spain.*

Archeological Museum: La Dama de Elche *sits tall and monumental, life size, despite the fact that she is 2500 years old. She gazes straight ahead, her dark hair pulled up in combs in a style still used today in the south of Spain. She is the first Sevillian woman, two millennia ahead of her time. With her beautiful* mantilla *(scarf), her dark hair and strong nose, she could have stepped out of last year's photograph of the traditional Holy Week celebration. In fact, she is a burial urn, containing her own ashes. I can tell from the work that she was loved and revered, a holy woman from ancient Iberia.*

At the Art Museum by Laura

A bright pink flower and a bright pink bird, splashing color onto the stormy mountains. Bird and flower sing fragile, handle-with-care songs, but those water balloon clouds don't seem to be listening. Helpless, they wait for the clouds to pop and the wind to roar and gobble them up. So small, so beautiful, so colorful, they wait.

A child watches the sea. It rolls, a fascinating jumble of green and blue and purple, and bubbly white at the edges. The bubbles reach their fingers out to her, pleading her to throw off her shoes and let the cold climb up her feet. Laughing shrieks from barefoot children tug at her legs, willing her to come in and play. But she tells them not now, because right now she is very busy. Right now, she's tying the sand and the sea and the sky into one big bow on the back of her dress.

Gray shards of reality mash together. Somewhere, an orange slice moon washes the world in blue strokes of light. Sometimes, a hand flies over an instrument's neck, bathing the world in music. Or maybe the moon plays the music and the hand paints the light, and all around them, reality bends lines into geometric shapes. Where and when are thrown away, here is there, and now is never. Time has gotten confused and is running circles around a musician, who plays lonely songs under the moonlight.

How still everything is. Not a leaf flutters or a wave crashes. Even light stops moving. Everything is caught mid-thought, mid-storm, mid-song, all stopped by a paintbrush. Each painting is a world on pause, and I'm free to explore every detail, until I could slip into the canvas. Until I could jump in next to the bird and the flower and feel dizzy because we're right on the edge of the mountain and the ground is so far away. And when I leave the museum, my whole world is moving a little slower, and it seems like everything is just waiting to be painted.

GRACIOUS HOSPITALITY IN MOROCCO

We fell in love with the Moorish art, architecture and culture that suffuse southern Spain even now, seven hundred years after the Moors were expelled from the Spanish peninsula. Wanting to trace the roots of this culture, we followed the scents of cumin and mint down into Morocco for two weeks in the month of October. On our itinerary were the wonderful cities of Marrakech, Casablanca, Fez, Tangiers, and the capital city of Rabat. Each was different and more wonderful than the last. We visited with our friends Leila and Souki and their families in the coastal town of Mohammedía, near the much more famous Essaouira. We also spent some time hiking in the Atlas Mountains. Two weeks was not nearly enough.

Leila and Souki had stayed with us for several weeks in an exchange program with our local high school the previous year. While they were visiting, Leila came down with a serious illness and had to be hospitalized. The crisis brought our families together and I will never forget Leila, Souki or the teacher with whom they traveled, Laure. They are all fellow travelers in our lives.

In Morocco, we spent time with the teachers, the students and their families. Leila's family was very gracious in showing us an insider's view of Rabat. Their teacher, Brahim, showed us his Casablanca, and we accompanied Laure and her son up into the Atlas Mountains on foot to visit the tiny village where she has created a service program. She brings her students from the city to help this low-income rural community develop jams which they sell as artisanal products, creating bonds between urban affluence and rural subsistence life.

Prior to our trip, the prevailing wisdom was this: don't go to Morocco without a guided tour. It's dangerous, they said. You could get sick; you could be robbed. The merchants will take advantage of you and make you buy things you don't want. Only dear Rick Steves chatted about venturing on a trip without a tour group. Well if Rick can do it, with his uneven French, we can certainly do it. That's what I thought to myself.

In retrospect, the concerns we heard and absorbed about Morocco were related to its non-Western culture. There is no small trace of anti-Islamic sentiment involved. I have to own my sharing that attitude, never having visited a country in the Arab region before. However, the majority of Morocco's citizens are Amazigh by origin and speak one of the Berber languages, with Arabic a second language for many. French is widely spoken as well. So calling it an Arab country would be inaccurate. Nevertheless, the prejudice remains. As I share below, we did have some experiences that stirred up those stereotypes. But everywhere there is poverty, one can feel threatened. As well we should. We have resources, and most others don't. I am very glad we went to Morocco, giving our family an opportunity to confront these prejudices head-on in ourselves.

Morocco was gorgeous, fascinating and challenging. There is poverty that hits you hard and makes you realize that you are one of the lucky ones, one of the ones assured of enough food and a bed to sleep on every night. Yet there is a large middle class with a high level of education whose members have chosen to live in Morocco because they prefer it there. The climate, the food, the architecture, the rich culture: there is much to adore in Morocco. We were lucky to be hosted by Leila's family when we arrived. Their generosity and warmth provided us an instant feeling of visiting family, in a place that might have felt very foreign. This made our travel much easier and more educational. Trips to Rabat, Casablanca and Mohammedía on the Atlantic coast were sandwiched between evenings discussing politics, eating phenomenal local food and learning about Moroccan history, culture and current politics.

Najib and Leila (father and daughter) share their birthday party

Our stay was too short to unravel many of the mysteries we encountered in Morocco. First, the absence of road signs in the *medinas,* the ancient city centers, made it nearly impossible for us to find our way, and we were continually disoriented. We used the good maps in the Lonely Planet and Dorling Kindersley guides, but we wished we had brought along a compass. We ended up hiring people to lead us places, either by car or on foot. There is no shortage of offers for tourist assistance, and this allowed us to support local people.

In the cities, the mixture of different peoples with a wide variety of clothing styles seemed mysterious to us. What do the different styles indicate about the individual? Some men wear a long dark blue *jellaba* robe with attached hood, pointed at the top. Male water sellers wear huge pointed multicolored hats, looking like tourists just back from Mexico, with matching multicolored short skirts and tunics. They clang their metal cups and offer water to passersby. Women wear many different levels of veils, from the loose *chador* scarf to the *niqab*, a covering leaving only a slit for the eyes. We saw an old woman who sat all day at the tomb of a 17th century saint in Casablanca. We came back later in the day and she was still there. She seemed to be worshiping the saint, not collecting tips. Why was she there all day? So many mysteries.

When we traveled in the *medinas*, several people said to us that visitors must not go to certain areas, since they are closed to foreigners. Others disagreed, saying that there are no closed areas. Which is true? We never did find out. Non-Muslims are not generally invited to enter mosques in Morocco (apparently due to the disrespectful attitudes of French soldiers during their occupation). Therefore we were ready to believe that certain neighborhoods might be closed, and we were willing to comply with such an injunction. But in fact, the opposite happened. Walking around the neighborhood, a guide approached us and offered to show us some of the workshops in the medina. He took us to a metal workshop and introduced us to an employee who was eager to tell us about his way of life. The metalworker took us up the winding stairs to a tiny attic bedroom, with only a bed covered in graying sheets, the smell of hot metal filling the air. "This is where I live," he said happily. He and his compatriots were preparing their noon-time meal over a brazier on the floor of the workshop. He was clearly proud of the work he was doing. Another man, whom we saw only at a distance, had a job that tore at our heartstrings even more. His job was to wade in camel and pigeon urine, processing hides to produce leather belts and purses for tourists. How can this job be acceptable work for anyone?

A worker tanning leather in Fez

Another mystery to us was the negotiation, or *marchandise*, that has to be done to purchase almost anything in Morocco. It is disorienting not to know either the ceiling or the floor price when looking at an item. There is no such thing as idly looking at a price tag. Asking the merchant how much he wants for something (there were very few female merchants) changes your status from disinterested tourist to active participant in the buying game. Once you have requested a price, you are often invited to sit in the back room drinking mint tea, to discuss exactly what you are looking for and to wait while the most desired product is brought from downstairs, or across town for that matter, for your inspection. It is hard to disengage from this encounter without having bought something. We found the best way to deal with this situation was with humor, patience and a certain amount of detachment. There was much laughter and joking about price and values, and a sense of goodwill was generated when we connected with the sellers on a personal basis. And at the end of the exchange, we knew that if we had paid too much, it was only a small gift to someone who needed the money far more than we.

We arrived in Morocco by boat from Spain and then headed down the coast to Mohammedía, where we met our dear friends. We had decided to rent a car, thinking that it would be easier and cheaper for a family of five. That was a poor decision. The car was a rental from Europcar, which sounded safer to our Eurocentric ears. We had to laugh at ourselves after we had set out, to find that the car had a slow leak in one tire as well as faulty windows. That slow leak was the bane of our driving experience in Morocco, as it prevented us from leaving the main highways for fear of having a flat tire out in the country. It would have been far better to have taken the grand taxis, huge old Mercedes vehicles that travel long distances as well as navigating the cities. Even the trains would have been better than that old rental car. The take-away message for me? Caution can get in our way.

Some mental snapshots from Morocco:

Sleeping in a riad, *a traditional home/hotel in the old quarter on our first night in Tangiers, I listened to a continual soundtrack all night long. Buyers and sellers, horse-drawn wagons pulling produce, young people partying, dogs barking and babies crying. Early in the morning I looked out the window to see the street sellers setting up their wares. Others, not as well-housed as we, stepped out of tents that had been set up on the roof of the market, stretched, and greeted the day.*

The Hassan II Mosque in Casablanca, *with millions of tiny tiles, all handmade, inlaid into gorgeous mosaic walls. On the lower level were forty-two enormous and intricately designed stone fountains where eight hundred worshippers could cleanse their hands, face and feet at the same time in preparation for prayers.*

The Jma el Fna Square in Marrakech, *with smoke rising from hundreds of fires in the center where* tajine *(a savory casserole), kebabs, and couscous are sold every night. The buildings are lighted around the huge square, giving the impression of an enormous party for thousands. Around the dark edges, however, mothers send their young children to ask the tourists for spare change.*

Driving in the medina in Marrakech at dusk, we became completely disoriented. We explained our predicament to a passerby in French, a man on a motorcycle heading home from work. He offered to lead our car to its destination. We followed him as closely as we dared, as he wove among pedestrians, animals, cars and trucks, leading us on a labyrinthine trail through the medina. He had to stop and wait for us numerous times, as we were not as bold as he. Once we had to jam on our brakes as we came through a tunnel around a corner and found two young boys on bicycles speeding headlong in our direction. He took us well out of his own way and did not leave us until we had arrived safely. He refused to accept a gratuity in thanks.

An encounter in Fez: *As I struggled to park the car within centimeters of the wall to avoid being hit on the narrow street, an old woman approached the car asking for alms. She was well dressed and carried a basket. "La, la",*

I muttered in my rudimentary Arabic, "No, no." I was in a rush and I do not normally give money to individuals. In the United States, I generally contribute to organizations that serve the poor, not to individuals who might spend the money on drink or drugs. However, the woman gave me a look which indicated she was not used to being turned down, particularly on a Friday, the day of worship. Her look needed no translation, "You are going straight to hell, young lady!" I quickly found some coins for her.

A family in Fez drawing water from a community fountain

Visiting the ancient ruins of Chellah outside Rabat. *The old Roman and Phoenician city, now abandoned, was filled with vines, Roman columns, stray cats and 15th century pools and aqueducts. It reminded me of pictures I've seen of Angkor Wat in Cambodia, so regal and melancholy.*

Hiking in the High Atlas Mountains along a mountain path, we saw nothing around us but sheep herders, snow-capped peaks and tiny villages down below, made entirely of stone and adobe. On the narrow paths shy travelers passed us leading donkeys carrying loads of vegetables from their terraced gardens, or stone for construction. One night, our friends invited us up to the roof with an invitation: "Venez voir les étoiles de la terre!" "Come see the earth stars!" We followed him up the winding staircase, not knowing what to expect. Bright shining in the velvety dark night were the "earth stars", the only five electric lights visible as far as the eye could see, even in this treeless mountain range. We had never felt so far removed from city life.

Our young friend hitched a ride on the burro carrying the water supplies while we hiked

Sleeping in an olive orchard belonging to a friend of a friend, outside Marrakech. They have worked on the property for several years, adding sleeping and eating quarters to a very simple terrain, or farm. They started by putting in a beautiful swimming pool which they share with their neighbors. Then they added a simple outdoors kitchen, a dining and living area with fireplace for cold nights, several sleeping tents and cottages and a bathroom building, fully plumbed. Wooden walkways join the separate living spaces. The style is simple, yet everything one would need is provided, in a spirit of generous Moroccan hospitality.

Laure preparing dinner in the "kitchen"

Listening to the muezzin, *the calls to prayer from each mosque, that sound five times per day. The prayer starts with a sonorous male voice singing "Allah Akbar" and continues for several minutes. In Marrakech, we stayed within earshot of five or six different mosques. The calls were staggered, with some ending after others had started up, so the sound went on for a good fifteen minutes. Someone told me that it is not only a call to prayer, but actually a prayer being sung as well. Hearing a prayer being sung through the city at five in the morning is a wonderful way to wake up.

Scarves: *Laura and I wear scarves every day this autumn, and they take on different uses and meanings as the months go by. On the Camino, coming into town with dusty clothes from hiking all day, a scarf was useful to throw around my neck to disguise my dirty shirt and provide a hasty transition to suitable dinner attire. When we visited a church in warm weather, we carried large sarongs to turn our shorts or sleeveless shirts into skirts and long-sleeved blouses. Spain is still a conservative country in many ways, and strongly Catholic.*

In Morocco, scarves are everywhere. Women wear varying styles of hijab, sometimes chosen strictly for fashion, coupled with fine makeup and stiletto heels. Some women cover themselves completely except for a slit opening for the eyes, the niqab. Even those who do not wear a traditional veil often wear a scarf around the neck. One rarely sees a female knee or elbow in Morocco. Laura and I found it natural to follow this trend, wearing long pants or skirts along with a scarf around our shoulders. Somehow we felt that we stood out a bit less as tourists in this way.

When we got back to Madrid, scarves seemed to be everywhere as a fashion accoutrement. Women of all ages wore scarves around their necks on the streets: wool, fur, cotton, matching or not. Men too wore scarves, sometimes the Palestinian kuffiyeh, identified with the Palestinian rights movement. These scarves are popular worldwide, and many are now made in China. I understand that Urban Outfitters have put one in their clothing line. They are calling it a "Hound's-Tooth Desert Scarf". The kuffiyeh is still a symbol of support for the Palestinian cause, but this may be changing. It seems to be morphing into a men's fashion accoutrement with a somewhat exotic look and nothing more. Around the world, we are all starting to dress more alike. Apparently, we are also forgetting why we wear what we wear.

Books could and probably have been written on the art of choosing and tying scarves in urban Europe. Laura and I knew little about the fashion directives for scarf wearers. Wraps and French twists were not our specialty. All we knew was a quick throw around the neck or a covering the shoulders for the cool evening walk back home from visiting the Prado. They quickly became irreplaceable as the weather cooled and our cotton clothes needed a little extra warmth.

Clothing is complicated. It identifies the wearer and points out fashion flaws. More important, it identifies us according to political affiliation, nationality, and even what is closest to one's heart, our personal faith. Observant Catholic or disrespectful traveler ogling parishioners in sacred cathedrals? Modest Muslim woman, observant or not? Palestinian political sympathizer or ignoramus? Fashionable woman or oblivious tourist? It is amazing that the same small item of clothing has so many interpretations.

Souks in Morocco by Conor

One of the amazing experiences while in Moroccan cities are the souks, or markets. Although sometimes it's easy to get lost, they are a great way to see the culture and walk around the city. There are many little shops selling all sorts of items ranging from fresh dried fruit, to bracelets and jewelry, to hand knotted rugs. The store owners are usually nice, and if you try, you can see the tea pot full of mint tea, the drink of Morocco, hidden in a little corner. This is a great place to go shopping.

If you go into a store, you'll notice there aren't price tags on the items. This is because the price is up for negotiation. Before asking what the item is being sold for, determine a number in your mind of the most you would pay for it. Keep this in mind as you negotiate. Most importantly, remember to keep a positive attitude. Treat it as a game as the sellers do, and enjoy it. That makes it fun!

Morocco is an enchanting country. It is filled to the brim with natural beauty, fascinating and diverse cultures, and of course, many of the people speak French, one of the most beautiful languages in the world. I could easily understand why international citizens Karine and Ahmed have built their quiet retreat in an olive grove there, and why my friend Laure, a French citizen and schoolteacher, chooses to make her home in Morocco. Both the food and the weather are excellent, and like anywhere, a person with enough money can enjoy all that the country has to offer. It is true that political freedom is limited, since Morocco is ruled by a monarch. I experienced the arbitrary nature of this power one day when I drove onto one of the monarch's properties by mistake, being lost again. It looked like *a public park. A soldier approached my car and immediately "fined" me 700 dirhams (about $100) to be paid on the spot. Lucky for us, he was on foot. That and speaking French ("So sorry – it won't happen again", was what I think I said as I turned the car around quickly) saved us an extra donation to the monarchy. The king doesn't need our small change, as apparently he owns 6% of the country's GDP.*

Yet with all that Morocco has to offer, I could see why Marrakech is the new hotspot for glitterati worldwide. With its abundant sunshine, it looks like Palm Springs, but with much more style. Both past French Presidents Jacques Chirac and François Sarkozy have homes there, as well as a number of international glitterati. I kept looking for Brad Pitt in Marrakech, but we didn't see him. Instead, we got to know a bit about a fascinating and colorful country, one that continues to harbor many mysteries for me. I would return in a heartbeat to learn more.

VISITING OLD AND NEW FRIENDS IN KENYA

As the autumn went on, we became increasingly unmoored from the academic schedule. People rushed to work or walked their dogs. We visited museums and wandered through the many ethnic neighborhoods and down the huge boulevards of Madrid. Exploring the streets in the late fall, we had to supplement our lightweight wardrobes (a few items only, chosen mainly by weight) with gloves and extra socks or stockings. When the snow flurries flew in the Parque El Retiro, we knew it was time to head south in our quest to follow the autumn season all year long.

The kids and I flew to Kenya in early December, an infrequent flight on our slow travel year. It was a long trip, made longer by the obligatory stop in London on the way. Though its colonial claims on Kenya are long gone, Great Britain's ties to this country are still strong. So to fly from Spain to Kenya we had to go by way of London, nearly 800 miles to the north. Longer still was the cultural distance between Madrid and rural western Kenya. In Kenya, we traveled mainly in the Western Highlands area, where we already had a number of ties. As usual, we decided to visit the people with whom we had connections. Our Quaker community formed our strongest connections. Quakers are more numerous in Kenya than anywhere else on earth, ever since the first decade of the twentieth century when Quaker missionaries fanned out from the United States, bringing Quaker practices to Africa and to Central and South America. In Kenya, many Quaker communities were founded such that each one was no more than a day's walk to the next.

Our first stop was the city of Kakamega, where we visited a Quaker-based AIDS orphanage that we had been supporting with donations. Once we met the children in person, they stole our hearts. The orphanage is a project of a group of New England Quakers in partnership with Kenyan Quaker women. Our visit coincided with the start of the holidays, and we expected a small group of children. However, when we arrived, forty children came out to greet us. We were expecting to provide full-time recreational programming for the children during our visit, and we had come prepared with a duffle bag full of craft projects, soccer balls, Frisbees, writing supplies and the like. Our small group of four visitors made this a challenging project. However, the kids were incredibly patient with us and happy with whatever little we were able to provide. We shared Christmas card design, creative writing projects, singing, and playing soccer and Frisbee. The Kenyan and New England students were fascinated to learn from each other. Unexpected projects came up too, including taking portraits of each child to offer them as a keepsake. In Kenya, digital cameras are still rare and the traveling portrait artist still finds employment. The kids were happy to have a formal portrait made and kept it among their prize possessions.

In Kakamega, we also visited the home of Mercy, an exchange student who had lived with us while she attended college. It was meaningful to spend time with her family and to offer them anecdotes about their daughter who had been absent for several years. We also spent time with friends in the Amesbury for Africa program. Amesbury, a nearby community in Massachusetts, has chosen Esabalu, a village of eighty-five hundred rural inhabitants in western Kenya, as its sister community. We were able to bring donations to the program activists and help build the sister community relationship by forging new connections with these inspiring people and programs. To round out our trip, we took a few days off for a visit with the wild animals at Maasai Mara Game Reserve, on the way back to Nairobi.

Mercy's extended family

One of the benefits of visiting Kenya as a Quaker is the large number of Quakers who live there. The Grace family from the United States made their home in Kenya for a number of years. Eden is a faithful member of the administrative team that works hand in hand with Kenyan Quakers on many development projects, from hospitals to schools to women's microenterprise programs. She was living with her husband and their two boys in Kisumu, a city between Kakamega and Nairobi. Eden helped us immeasurably with our detailed plans for visiting Kenya and her family welcomed us into their home for a couple of days. In some ways, it was like a trip back to the States, with online access, home movies and more comfortable living quarters than we had experienced until then. They were very generous, inviting us to share in Christmas parties and church services along with their other daily activities.

From my journal:

Children's Care Centre, Kakamega: *This week we are living at the Children's Care Centre, a home for children orphaned by AIDS. Kenyan Quaker women founded the Centre with the assistance of New England Quakers, in 2001. The Kenyan women had noticed children coming to their church service in search of food, and realized that many of them had no families, since their parents had died. Many of them were living completely by themselves in empty houses. This motivated the women to take on the enormous task of building an orphanage for the children. New England Quakers founded Friends of Kakamega, a US non-profit organization, to support this wonderful program.*

The Care Centre currently houses about fifty children aged 6 to 17. The staff members, many of whom who live full-time at the Centre, work tirelessly to promote a caring, family-like environment. They maintain connections with the school and with the extended family and neighbors, encouraging the children to maintain these relationships so that they will not lose contact with their community of origin. These visits also serve to maintain the children's right to return eventually to their home if they are lucky enough to have inherited one. But their real home is at the Care Centre. Our visit happened after school had ended for the Christmas break but before the children had left for the holidays. Many of them did not seem in a hurry to return to their families.

With expectations high, each minute is filled. Every morning our family holds a caucus to plan the day and each of us takes on a different activity, surrounded by a group of kids. We play, sing, offer arts and crafts programs, and introduce the kids to Frisbee. Always there is hair braiding for Laura ("Your hair is so soft!") and earnest exchanges of information among teens. One day we had a huge Frisbee and "football" (AKA, soccer) festival at the local park, where all the school's neighborhood children joined in, along with the cows.

Evan surrounded by friends at the Care Centre

What is most remarkable here is the caring that the children show for each other. The staff encourages them to work out their problems with each other like brothers and sisters, which they seem to do almost without exception. They are patient, waiting for hours until we are ready to present an activity to them. It's hard to believe that they are the children who are missing parental care. Their generosity is especially remarkable among children who have so little: each of them owns only one outfit of clothing and one small backpack with a few personal possessions.

At the Care Centre, the kids all get three square meals a day, staff who are committed to their care and lots of close friends who are like siblings to them. They are materially well off by the standards of most Kenyans. But they are lacking many things we take for granted: hot water, several changes of clothes and even a towel. I wake up each morning to the sounds of kids singing and laughing as they clean up in the yard using a bucket of water. Afterwards they stand on the porch, shivering and drying off in the morning sunlight. Though the air feels subtropical to our northern blood, the kids' hands are like ice.

As I was setting up my mosquito net over my bed on the first night, I heard gales of laughter down the hall in one of the girls' dorm rooms. Four girls share the room, and Laura was in their midst, telling stories and hearing their jokes and stories back. They call her the "smiley machine."

We have to be observant to try to make sure that we are not given too much, or better quality, than the others. It took us a day to realize that the bathroom next to our room, usually available for all, had been cleared out for our use alone. We had to persuade the staff that we did not need this luxury. At mealtimes, we seem to get a different quality of food and we are served separately. We are not sure whether this is due to our dietary needs (the Kenyan staff try to prevent North Americans from getting sick by offering only cooked food and bottled water) or to deference to the foreign visitors. Old habits die hard.

I lent the kids my camera and they took great candid shots of each other, clowning around. These pictures are so different from the serious formal poses that Kenyans typically strike in front of the camera. Picture-taking is still a serious portraiture business in Kenya. Portrait artists set up shop even at outdoors events, with an instant camera and battery-operated printer, so people can see their "snaps" right away. People pose in front of the Kenyan flag or a fictional jungle scene. Having your portrait taken is a luxury. Thinking back to the photo of our exchange student, Mercy, before she arrived, I remembered how severe she looked and how I had wondered, prior to meeting her, whether her personality would be equally severe. Her face was probably just reflecting the gravity of the important portrait being made.

Some of the most gifted singers among the children put on a concert at the regional Quaker meeting. They sang of their lives and recited together an affirmation they had learned at the Care Center: "It is difficult to live in this world. Some people look at me as a useless creature. Yet they do not know that I am a human being like them, created in the image of God." When I heard their voices ring out with this speech in the huge assembly room, I knew that they believed it to their core, and that good work was being done at the Care Centre.

Kakamega Rain Forest: *Today we met Job Ilondanga, who works as a guide at the Kakamega Rain Forest. It is a gorgeous forest in the middle of the Western Province, near the equator. The green trees appeared suddenly as we approached, a quiet oasis among the small farms and villages of the Maragoli Hills in Kenya, one of the most densely populated agricultural areas in the world. Job showed us colobus monkeys, many species of birds and a cave where fruit bats live. The cave was dug by hand in a vain attempt to look for gold in the 1820s. After walking straight back into the hill for forty meters, we came on the bats hanging from the ceiling. We woke them with our flashlights, and they rushed by our heads with a whoosh of air. Not a place for people with a fear of spiders, bats or small spaces.*

Job has dedicated himself to restoring the rain forest and educating people about it. With his earnings as a private guide, he visits schools and community groups, training them about forest ecology. He is restoring a forest corridor by planting trees that he is growing in his own nursery.

Lubau Village Meeting: *Another day we were invited to attend a new Quaker church. Four metal walls had been constructed in a field; no floor had yet been built. The children of the church performed songs, dances and stories to tell us about their lives and faith. One of them was a comical story about a family in which the father comes home drunk, and the women and children stand up for their rights. AIDS was discussed openly, much to our surprise. The boy acting the role of the father seemed to have a deep familiarity with the scene. Though his acting was hilarious, it was a poignant moment.*

Esabalu, Amesbury's sister community: *Laura and I are staying at Sherry's house, and Conor and Evan are staying with Priscilla and Jacopo, down the lane. We are in the small village of Esabalu, sister community to Amesbury, a city near our home. The two homes are very well kept; lovely gardens, flowering trees and tidy lawns surround each house. Just outside our bedroom door, two hens are being allowed to hatch their own eggs in the hall. They sit calmly and quietly, hardly moving. Outside our window is the animals' shelter, housing the cows and the dogs which protect the property. Sherry's nephews cut grass for the cows, which are on the no-grazing regimen. They stay in the yard and eat grass that is* cut for them daily, requiring the young men to work about three hours per day providing food for them. Apparently the benefits of limiting grazing are many, including healthier cows with less disease, more milk and a concentrated availability of compost. It's an interesting contrast: in the United States we love the romantic—and bucolic—image of free-range cows, while farmers in rural Kenya are moving in the opposite direction.

Our hosts are very courteous and kind. We are offered strong Kenyan tea whenever we go to see someone new. (The recipe for Kenyan tea involves boiling it for 10 minutes, then adding lots of milk and sugar. Mr. Twining must be rolling over in his grave, but it is delicious!) We are introduced to practically everyone in the village, though we will never be able to remember all their names. Their names are hard for us, as are ours for them. Conor has become Collins, a name that is familiar to them. Evan's name is generally pronounced "Even" but he doesn't mind. Actually, this name suits his temperament well.

I can tell that Sherry is a strong and effective community organizer. One of the main Kenyan organizers for Amesbury for Africa, she coordinates local action on the water project, the tree nursery, the health center, and many other projects besides. She watches the boys playing soccer with a critical eye, and she tells me she will not hesitate to correct a child who needs it. Children are raised by the whole community in the traditional way here, though she admits that this is changing recently, as teens are becoming more resistant to authority. Outside her outhouse she has a "tippy tappy", a cleverly designed water dispenser for cleaning hands. You step on the stick which is placed to tip the plastic water jug just enough to send a stream of water down. She is promoting this concept in the village as an important sanitation device. She is very good at bringing resources and people together. We see evidence of her work all around the community.

One difference between Kenyan and Moroccan women: in Morocco, the hamman, or baths, are a place of retreat and relaxation. Women go to the hamman to clean and pamper their bodies, to breathe the warm air of relaxation, and to visit with their friends. I do not see such an option for Kenyan women. Women in Kenya universally work very hard. They are up before dawn to clean the livestock areas, feed the chickens, sweep *the dirt floors, milk the cows, and prepare breakfast. They work all day taking care of the children, preparing all the meals, bringing water from the spring (five times a day up the muddy path), sweeping, and farming. The Quaker women we met attend their conferences and prayer groups in addition to their regular jobs. Walking down the roads, we frequently see groups of women representing different faiths. They stand out in their freshly cleaned matching dresses and head scarves. It is widely known that Kenyan women are the ones who do more of the work, and the ones to trust with money as well.*

We were able to reduce the load for the few days we were at Esabalu, helping to carry water, do some washing, and harvest the beans for seeds. Out walking early one morning to where Evan and Conor were staying, I crossed the lane, went through the corn field, and passed the barn to Priscilla's yard where I almost fell over in surprise. The boys were standing in the yard, washing tablecloths in a tub. All before breakfast! Mud was thick all over their shoes. This alone was surprising as they both tend to be very careful with their footwear. The scene was so far from what they would have been doing had they been at home that I had to laugh.

After washing, they were instructed to give the soapy water to the cows, who loved it. Not even that was wasted. I'll keep the image of the black and white cows, with their noses deep in the soap suds in the brilliant morning sunlight.

Sherry was up early tending the cow. I went out in the pre-dawn darkness and saw a hibiscus flower blooming in the yard. There were no stars since the cloud cover was complete, and there were no lights anywhere in the village. It was completely dark except for the white petals, and completely quiet. Our friends say electricity is coming soon to rural villages like Esabalu. For now, some have a small solar unit to power their cell phones, the only electricity being used. These compact units have five or six ports and can accommodate all the cell phones in the household. As of now, the cell phone penetration rate in Kenya is 64 per 100 people, compared to 91 per 100 in the United States. But it is rising rapidly. Those without a solar charger go to public kiosks in town for their "charge up" as well as their "top up", paying for additional minutes. Kerosene lamps are used in the homes here in the village. In the larger city of Kakamega, on the other hand, electricity and running water are widespread.

Evan and Conor doing the washing

Will the developing world have to make the same mistakes as we in the developed countries have made in resource use, chewing up non-renewable resources in their mania to have the modern conveniences? Clearly, the fabric of our earth cannot sustain this. Something will have to give. Perhaps they will jump ahead of us, inventing innovative solutions that are more sustainable and will show us all a better way. We already see this in the mobile banking system in Kenya, where money is exchanged via SMS messages on cell phones, obviating the need for bank branches and reducing the need to travel around to make or collect payments.

In rural Kenya one can still see that energy use is much lower than in North America. With no electricity or running water, almost everything is made by hand. Packaged bread and juice are brought out only for visitors, while our hosts generally purchase unprocessed foods which they cook on a charcoal or wood brazier. We eat the chickens raised in the yard. The markets are an efficiently designed processor for goods discarded by the developed nations. T-shirts, shoes, magazines and other items that we all donate are sorted and sold according to a carefully defined system of value. Within the market, there are separate streets for used clothing, shoes, cooking pots, hardware items, and rehabilitated electronics. But will people in the developing world always be content to use our leftovers?

Snapshots from Nairobi: *John has a cousin who is a Maryknoll priest. Father Dick invited us to visit with him for the evening while we were in Nairobi. He has worked for many decades teaching film-making to youth groups, and he is now retired. Despite its current role as a retirement home for priests, the Maryknoll Center is a place of vibrant progressive energy. Bookcases are full of reports on current development projects, and there is a constant flow of visitors whose work brings them to Nairobi. There is a friendly, informal style to the place. We were surprised to see the living room stocked with many of the comforts of home: salted cashews on the coffee table, and gin and tonics on offer, complete with ice. "What's your poison?" he asked as he opened the liquor cabinet. I thought I had entered a time machine, and had arrived back in a genteel and friendly home from the 1960s. Father Dick and his compatriots are die-hard Yankee fans and follow all the games with a level of enthusiasm unmatched outside of New York. For a little while that evening, we felt like we were back in the States.*

One day we visited the Kazuri Bead workshop. This organization was started in the 1980s to provide employment to women who are single parents. We toured the building where they work, making beautiful beads which have become high-end fashion accessories in the West. I closed my eyes at one point, taking in the happy sounds of women talking to each other, sitting and making clay beads. Talk, high energy and laughter filled the air. The sun poured in. The beads themselves are gorgeous, and the company's order chart is filled with requests from all over Europe and the United States.

A friend of a friend told us about the Lotus Pre-School in the Kibera slum. We were the first visitors to the school, as it had opened only two weeks previously. Kibera is the largest slum in Nairobi, and probably the largest in Africa, though its exact population is unknown. Only twenty percent of the inhabitants have electricity, and there is neither a public sewerage system nor other government services. Instead there is a huge maze of shacks, most tiny and housing many inhabitants each. We hopped from stone to stone along the "street" to get to the school, the stepping stones providing some partial separation from the open sewer that meandered down the center of the alleys. Once inside, we were greeted by well-dressed pre-school children playing "Follow the Leader" and singing for us on a clean concrete floor, with posters and plastic chairs all around. We taught them "If you're happy and you know it", leaving out the sad and angry parts. The school was impressive. However, the day nearly ended badly. Our driver said that while he was waiting for us, the car was surrounded by several young men with sticks, interested in what was inside. He almost drove away without us. So many people are filled with desperation here.

One day we visited the Sheldrick Elephant Orphanage, near Nairobi National Park. Incredibly, the park is just west of the airport, very close to downtown Nairobi. It was started as a response to the massive poaching that was taking place in the 1970s. Elephants are raised under the protection of the park and released to the wild as adults. When we arrived, the teenage elephants were being called in from where they live in the Park for lunch. They responded to the call by coming in at a run, ears flapping, eager for their milk. The trainers ran to provide it, holding the bottles upside down, and the teenage elephants guzzled the milk as fast as it could be provided. In the space of a few seconds, each elephant downed at least a gallon of milk, tossing the empty containers aside like spoiled children. What a handful it would be, traveling with children like those elephants!

On our way to the airport, we stopped at a fancy restaurant for dinner before leaving Kenya. Located on the main highway, it could have been a restaurant in a suburban strip mall in the States. A grand entrance stairway led upwards past neon lights advertising tropical scenes to an upstairs food court, discotheque, and an Indian restaurant overlooking the game park across the highway. It was the sort of establishment that would host a wedding or graduation party for a wealthy Kenyan family. As we ate our chicken korma, I noticed a vehicle moving slowly on the highway. Looking more closely, we saw two men navigating a pushcart filled with an enormous pile of cardboard boxes. One man was the driver, pulling the vehicle, while the other ran behind, alternately keeping a hand on the boxes so they would not fly away, and glancing behind to make sure they would not be hit by a faster-moving vehicle. It would be hard for a driver to see them at night, and there was no breakdown lane. The contrast inherent in these two scenes is surely typical, and I imagine one gets inured to them over time. I was glad to be shocked at the situation.

Teenage elephants having their milk

A safari in the Maasai Mara: *Having spent most of our two week stay in Kenya with Quaker communities and other friends, visiting and volunteering, we did not want to leave the country before taking a safari. After some research online, we hired a relatively inexpensive tour operator. This took some doing, as the safari industry in Kenya has figured out how to separate a fool from his money quite effectively. As it turned out, we may have been the fools on that score.*

Our tour operators drove us to the far western side of Kenya where it borders Tanzania. On the Tanzanian side is Serengeti National Park, and on the Kenyan side it is called Maasai Mara Game Reserve, where we chose to visit. We stayed in a campground with some amenities: big old-fashioned canvas tents with beds and bedding provided, and a bathroom with running water. It was luxurious camping. We were provided with beautiful hot meals: chicken and mashed potatoes with a tomato coriander sauce, and fresh fruit. Since it was the off season, we were the only guests. It was quiet and lovely.

We were camping deep in the forest, and the nights were very dark. Though the campground was surrounded by impenetrable thorn bushes, two Maasai men were assigned to stay awake outside all night protecting us from the lions. I heard their quiet talk in the dark, punctuated by long silences. Then came the unmistakable sound of lions roaring in the distance.

David owned the trip business and the van, but he had hired Dennis, a young Maasai man who had grown up in the village neighboring the reserve, to show him where the animals could be found. Dennis sat in front wearing his short red tunic and his clan's trademark yellow shawl with enormous red polka dots. He told us this fabric identified him as a young unmarried man. Dennis was still in boarding school, after which he hoped to attend university in Nairobi and become a surgeon. He was preceded by another young man in the village who is attending university now, the village's first university student. Dennis was home over the holidays with his mother only, since his older siblings were away at school.

On safari, the ordinary safari things happened. Our vehicle, like all the other vehicles safari vans in the park, and just like in the Disney movies, had a pop-up center section, allowing us to stand safely in the van with the best possible view of the animals. Except that when you see those magnificent animals up close—and unfenced—it is not ordinary. The stunning beauty of the animals, the diversity of all the different species, and the drama of their existence takes your breath away. It was an amazing trip, made even more memorable by an adventure that happened on the second day of our safari. We were parked near a group of lions (when one

*is near a group of lions, it is suddenly obvious why it is called a "pride").
All at once I had a sinking feeling, literally. The driver was trying to turn
around, but we had a flat tire. I suddenly remembered that the previous day
on the way into the park, the driver had stopped to have a tire inspected.
"No, don't replace the tire", I remember him saying. "Just patch it." That
might have been a poor decision. We were suddenly in a predicament, next
to a pride of lions busy chewing their cuds or whatever it is they do, but
looking like they could chew on some humans sometime soon.*

*David and Dennis had to figure out how to change the tire. People do
not get out of their vehicles in the safari park. It is simply not done, as
the animals are indeed wild and most are carnivorous. Of course we, the
tourists, were under strict instructions to stay put. Dennis unsheathed his
machete and put it on the ground in front of him, ready for action. Later,
when we learned that Dennis' father had been killed by a water buffalo in
the park, our feelings for him and his bravery increased even more.*

*There were several other safari vans in the neighborhood. Apparently
our show was more interesting than the lion show, since we noticed that
all the tourists had turned their binoculars from the lions to face our
direction instead. The drivers kindly formed a cordon with their vans
so as to protect our van from the lions' view. With help from another
driver, David and Dennis were eventually able to change the tire and
we went on our way. This experience made our safari trip even more
memorable—and I imagine Dennis did not soon forget it either. What
seemed to be a good deal on a safari led us to experience a bit of added
drama in the bargain.*

*Later, we visited Dennis' village, where we were impressed at the cultural
pride of the Maasai people. Maasai men can be seen all over western
Kenya, wearing their bold red, pink and purple cloaks. Their villages
surround the game reserve. The Maasai are wealthy in cattle and they
live very close to their animals; their simple mud huts are built in a circle
surrounded by thorn bushes, and at night the animals are brought into the
middle of the circle for safety. Calves and baby goats sleep in a room in
the hut with their masters. The Maasai alone among Kenyan tribes have
chosen to retain their traditional ways, relying very little on money or on
the dominant culture. Though I am glad not to have been invited to share*

their traditional diet of cow's blood, milk and meat, we all were so glad to have visited Dennis' village and to see his people's way of life. The image of tall Dennis with his shy smile and downy growth on his chin stays with me, and I pray that he is able to move through the modern world and bring back his training to help his people as he hopes to do.

HOME FOR CHRISTMAS

We all missed John. He had taken two trips to join us for short visits during our time abroad, first participating in part of our time in Spain, and then coming along as co-traveler and bodyguard in Morocco. But when we had planned the Big Trip, it was clear to all of us that nine months was a long time away from home. We missed being together as a family at home, and the kids were eager to see their friends. I was eager to check in with friends and family, particularly with my aging mother. And there was a great deal to be said for coming home for the holidays. So we incorporated a trip back to Massachusetts for a few weeks before starting out anew on the second leg of our journey.

The trip home worked out for logistical reasons as well. Remember the Camino? Well, we had each been carrying around two sets of equipment all fall: our large frame backpacks complete with hiking clothes, boots and rain ponchos, and one small rollaway suitcase. The suitcase held an incredibly small and compact collection of clothing, requiring us to do our laundry every week and to stay in relatively warm climates. We had been able to stow our packs in a few places along the way: with a friendly hostel owner in Madrid and in a friend's apartment. But the packs came along with us to Kenya where they were quite cumbersome, though useful on the safari. By the time we left Kenya, we were eager to jettison our packs and switch to our small suitcases. The young men in the Kibera slum in Nairobi could have easily relieved us of all of our luggage. The less stuff, the better, we had discovered.

Being home gave us some personal space, a welcome change for us all. At fourteen, sharing a bed with your mom gets old. Not that anyone had complained, of course. But we all breathed a sigh of relief to have a few weeks at home and a bit more personal space.

I polled the family to ask what was best about being home for the time over Christmas. Evan said it was the chance to work on silk-screening, a hobby of his that he hoped to share with kids in Latin America as well. For Conor, the best was to be able to drink water straight out of the tap. Laura appreciated hanging out with her cat. I loved skating on the clear black ice that we have once a year in New England, when we're lucky. Some people love watching eclipses. I love the exhilaration of flying across a lake in winter, and slowing down to watch the plant life move slowly in the frigid currents under the ice. Examining the living green plants under the frozen ice is like looking through a window on another world.

The main thing I noticed was that none of us wanted to quit the Big Trip. Everyone was given the opportunity to stay home, and we all wanted to continue with Part Two: Latin America. This would be the chance to put our Spanish to use on some longer-term volunteering projects and to engage on a deeper level with the host communities by focusing on two countries: Guatemala and Bolivia. We chose these two because we had both friends and volunteer possibilities in each, and because the level of need in both countries is among the highest in the Americas.

GUATEMALAN WINTER

We flew to Guatemala in January, escaping one of the snowiest winters in recent memory. Amidst overwhelming poverty, we found bougainvilleas filling our vision with their bright colors. Jacaranda cascading over high garden walls towards the street created a violet mist above us. We slept with the window open and the moonlight pooling on the floor. In the daytime, it was warm enough to consider swimming, though the opportunity rarely presented itself. We were busy with our volunteer work.

Guatemala meant putting our language training to use. We had researched programs online and communicated with a few of them, but the final choices of where we would volunteer were not yet made when we arrived. However, the basic outline was established. We would live in Antigua, a small city which is the hub for European and North American expats in Guatemala. Laura and Conor would take Spanish lessons in the morning with one of the many language schools. The afternoons would be reserved for volunteering with an after-school program. I would volunteer with a microfinance organization in the mornings and help out with the kids' program in the afternoons.

This schedule worked out well. On the weekends we took some trips by bus, once to build fuel-efficient stoves in a city called Xela with a Canadian couple we had met, and once to tour the gorgeous Lake Atitlán area. After two months in Antigua, we took a short trip to the Atlantic coast to visit the English-speaking Garífuna people.

We had some trepidation about choosing Guatemala. The US State Department website generally contains useful cautionary advice for travelers, but it does not help one to gain confidence about traveling abroad. The Guatemala description was truly discouraging. Guatemala has one of the highest murder rates in the world. Kidnappings and robberies of tourists and local residents are commonplace. The narrow isthmus of Central America serves as a conduit for drugs and crime, and the US-initiated war on drugs has pushed the drug trade south along this isthmus from Mexico well into Guatemala, the rest of Central America, and down into South America. The drug trade has only exacerbated the enormous issues stemming from class and ethnic conflict, political instability, and deep-seated poverty. Despite the incredible beauty of its landscape and warmth of its people, many potential visitors have avoided Guatemala in recent years.

As much as we wanted to volunteer in a place where we would be needed, I did not want to subject my family to danger. Blond teenagers stand out on a city bus. Even if we were lucky enough to avoid being targets of violence, I did not want to live in a place where we would have to carry around anxiety and fear all the time. Weighing the risks against the benefits of going to Guatemala, we decided after much deliberation that the city of Antigua, the old capital of Guatemala, would be our base of operations. It represented a realistic compromise for our family between living in a part of Guatemala which is thought to be risky for foreigners, and avoiding the country altogether.

Laura correctly described Antigua as "Disneyworld for progressives". It is a lovely city of walkable size with an easy-to-navigate grid pattern. The city was built by the Spanish in the sixteenth century, and it contains an unusual number of beautiful buildings, some well-kept and some in various degrees of scenic ruin. The streets are almost entirely cobblestone, which serves to slow the traffic and creates a quaint appearance. In the distance are several huge conical volcanoes that let out a frequent Disney-like puff of smoke but don't seem to threaten the city. (The innocent volcano is more myth than reality, unfortunately. Numerous lava flows have destroyed outlying villages and some upscale condominium developments near Antigua. In past centuries, lava has indeed reached Antigua itself and in fact caused the capital to be moved from Antigua to its current location in Guatemala City. What seems benign may not always be so.)

Colonial Antigua, ringed by active volcanoes

Indigenous women, many of whom live in the villages outside Antigua, come to the city for the day to sell their handmade fabrics to tourists. They wear gorgeous hand woven clothes with geometric designs and vibrant colors. Looking at these lush fabrics, one could almost forget the poverty and racism their owners experience daily. Yet the many social problems evident here in Guatemala present deep challenges in every community, and impressive work is being undertaken by a number of excellent non-profit organizations and the hordes of visiting foreigners. The coffee is fabulous; the restaurants are diverse and inexpensive. Flowers bloom and music flows out of public buses and free community concerts. Maybe staying in Antigua was a cop-out, but the compromise seemed to make sense for our family.

Besides being an absolutely gorgeous city, Antigua is a great place to learn Spanish. Not least because Guatemalan Spanish is one of the purest Spanish accents: clear and relatively slow, with few of the dropped consonants of speakers in other countries in Latin America. There are more language schools in Antigua than there are coffee shops, and that's saying something. We chose Proyecto Lingüístico Francisco Marroquín, a non-profit Spanish language school with a long history focused on linguistic research in the ancient Mayan languages.

Unlike other countries we visited, our Guatemalan contacts were made mostly through internet searching, not through any previous connections. I had explored locations and NGOs (non-governmental organizations, the term used to refer to non-profit organizations internationally) online during the year prior to our Big Trip. I had communicated with several organizations via email and Skype to learn about their work and consider where we would be best able to help. My Spanish language skills helped with this, though I could probably have made most of these connections in English. We decided to visit programs and make a decision later, although we arrived in Guatemala with some possibilities in mind.

By contrast, we preferred to set up detailed plans for the first few days in a foreign country. When traveling, we generally arrive tired and disoriented, a good target for thieves and those who take advantage of ignorant and comparatively wealthy tourists. I learned this the hard way many years ago when a thief pick pocketed my boyfriend in the subway on arrival in Paris. So when we arrived in Guatemala, we had arranged for a trusted taxi driver, found through colleagues at home, to take us to a specific language school where we had planned a home stay. Many of the language schools offer room and board to students, and we had decided to spring for this relatively expensive option for the first week.

The family, a couple with grown children, was very kind and lived in a large home with eight rooms to rent. They provided three hot meals a day and a warm welcome to Antigua. Having room and board taken care of for the first week allowed us the time to ease into living in Guatemala. While the young ones took their Spanish lessons, I made the acquaintance of some real estate agents and chose a house to rent. This was the only time on our Big Trip that we abandoned our rule not to stay in hotels or separate apartments on the open market, since there are not many home exchange opportunities in Guatemala. Not surprisingly, few Guatemalans can afford international vacations or second homes, so renting a house seemed the best route.

We found a cottage in a family compound near the center of the city, which turned out to be ideal. We became friends with our neighbors, and many Sunday afternoons were spent playing soccer with their kids. Our living space was more than adequate, with two bedrooms, a kitchen and living room, and a private garden. It was simpler living than most North Americans would accept at home, with a kitchen sink that left a puddle by the back door, a daily pile of termite dust in the living room, and minimal lighting. But we had electricity, hot water, and internet access. Even better, we lived in the community with our new friends, with whom we shared the drinking water delivery and experienced the rhythms of daily life. These included religious parades in the streets, roosters that woke us each morning, and firecrackers that Guatemalans enjoy setting off at all hours, for no particular reason than to celebrate life itself. After the first few nights, we learned not to tense up at each explosion, thinking it might be gunshots. For a rental fee of $400 a month, we were nicely settled in Guatemala.

Spanish school went on in the morning for several weeks. Both of the younger kids took private lessons with intensive grammar and conversation and daily homework assignments. It was a demanding schedule, and not something one would want to do every week, but for a few weeks it was a good way to cement their grammar and conversational skills. After visiting a few after-school programs, my three teens chose *Los Patojos* (meaning "The Kids") in the neighboring town of Jocotenango as their volunteer site. It was located in one of the highest-crime areas surrounding Antigua, so I accompanied them on the bus until they felt ready to go there on their own. The program was joyful, creative and educational. Evan helped with the teen program and Conor and Laura were welcomed to work with the younger kids.

Evan teaching guitar at Los Patojos – teen program

In addition to spending some time at Los Patojos, I chose to volunteer with Namaste, a women's microenterprise program. The program offers small loans, on the order of $200, which help low-income women to expand their businesses, such as selling tortillas, weaving fabric into gorgeous *huipiles* (traditional blouses), or raising chickens. In addition, the program offers financial education to help the women improve their business skills. Business advisors travel to the villages and meet with groups of borrowers, who learn how to keep track of expenses, how to attract and keep customers, and how to keep their business funds separate from their personal expenses (easier said than done). Micro-lending has become a hugely popular international development tool in the last ten years, but one that has seen its share of critics, due to rapid growth and inadequate regulation.

Despite its critics, there is no doubt that the popularity of micro-lending has helped increase international focus on very low-income women as important change agents in reducing poverty. The assumption is that resources that go to the mother help the entire family, whereas resources that go to the father are often spent on alcohol or cigarettes. Unfortunately, that is a basic socioeconomic truth around the world. Families where the mother has more education usually have fewer children, and the children are more likely to finish school. Though micro-lending has been criticized for offering only marginal employment to women, it definitely creates a positive impact on the household.

One of my favorite books in the microfinance field is *The International Bank of Bob*, by Bob Harris. Bob had invested his own funds in micro-lending groups through an organization called Kiva that uses crowdsourcing to bring financing from individuals in wealthy nations to small groups of borrowers in developing countries. He was interested in learning more about the people he was assisting, so he traveled all over the world and met with many of the people his small loans had helped. His definition of micro-lending is very apt: "Micro-lending helps a man who already knows how to fish by lending him some money to fix his boat."

My role with Namaste was to assess their programs, and in particular, to help rewrite their educational curriculum. I also piloted a program to measure the economic well-being of the families, a difficult task in a culture where hardly anyone has a bank account, where literacy and numeracy are limited, and where the chickens being raised to sell sometimes end up on the family's dinner table instead. I helped Namaste staff measure the results of their programs, using a simple tool called the Progress out of Poverty Index. This tool measures economic well-being with only ten questions, most of which can be observed visually in the home. Created by the Grameen Foundation, it has been used internationally and is very useful for assessing the impact of microfinance programs.

Two months in Guatemala flew by. John joined us for a visit once we had settled in, helping out at Los Patojos and joining us as we enjoyed getting to know Antigua's history and culture. He also accompanied me on my trips to the outlying villages, meeting some of the Namaste borrowers and experiencing my work in economic development.

Conor on life in Antigua:

For this round of contributions to the blog, I was asked to try to write something other than a short story. I was thinking about the difference between life at home and in Antigua, Guatemala. It's quite a touristy place, but in a sense that's a good thing. There's something to be said for familiarity, but another part of travelling is trying new things and widening one's comfort zone. With a TV, reliable internet and various other luxuries, I feel like it would be a stretch to say that life in Antigua is completely different from home.

Our stay in Antigua has shown us some of the reasons there are so many expats here. It felt like a place we could actually live in for longer than eight weeks. We're acquainted with our neighbors, and we like to say we know the town well. I've gotten used to living in our apartamentito, *or little apartment, and it seems like the differences between living here and at home are becoming less significant over time. It feels normal to walk three blocks to the supermarket. The city stretches only eight blocks from the north to south, and waking up in nice warm weather to the calls of exotic birds and a small patio bathed in sunlight is a delight.*

When we walk around the city, we notice that all the walls and doors are closed to the street, and there is no concept of a front yard. Each door is like a mysterious oyster waiting to be opened. It seems almost hostile, but the word "almost" lingers, like a soft pillow, assuring you that this crazy idea is far from the truth. Behind each door there may be a small family living in a tiny space, a wonderfully blooming garden or a long alleyway lined with plants splitting off into different houses.

Opposite this feeling, if you get on a bus for ten or twenty minutes, you end up in an area where almost everything is constructed out of worn, rusty corrugated metal. People cook with an open fire in the middle of the room. We tried to help a little with this problem by going to Xela (otherwise known as Quetzaltenango, place of the Quetzal bird) to build safe stoves with proper chimney pipes to let out the harmful smoke. In Antigua, we spend our afternoons at Los Patojos, volunteering and spending time with low-income Guatemalan kids in the program. Although I feel it seemed like there was not much to do at times, just sitting next to the kids while they work helps them concentrate and stay in their seats.

From my journal:

Kids at Los Patojos: *Their neighborhood is tough, yet the kids are so sweet. They approach us and ask for help with their homework and after-school projects. "Show me how you make a paper airplane!" several of them asked me. After I demonstrated the basic design and gave a little treatise on how you can alter the shape of the plane to improve its flight, a young girl came up to me. In her hand was a three-dimensional paper flower, the exact replica of a tulip. She offered it shyly to me by its paper stem. I was so glad to see her playful smile and the pride with which she showed it to me. We laughed together at the expertness of her work compared to the clumsy airplanes I was making. She sells these flowers on the street to make some money for her family. I guess she already knew something about origami.*

Conor likes to help out in the quiet room because it is quiet and cool. The children are supposed to work on their school work before they are released to the general chaos of the rest of the program. I, on the other hand, find it a sad place to be. The work is stupefyingly boring, with endless repetition the teaching method of choice in the local schools. After homework is done, however, the quiet room is a good place for respite from the crazy activity of seventy children playing in a small space. When I brought in a pack of playing cards, I soon found myself in a small group of pre-teen would-be card sharks. We sat in the cool back room and traded games. Go Fish, War and 21 are good ways to learn math and English vocabulary. Hopefully they won't be corrupted into a life of gambling as a result.

What drew us to Los Patojos is evident if you look at the wonderful photos on their website: the place is full of joy! Among the many NGOs focusing on after-school enrichment for low-income children, Los Patojos seems to be unique in encouraging children to be their most creative and joyful selves. The walls are covered with murals, children are encouraged to play ball and horse around during study breaks, and the sense of personal responsibility being taught reminds me of the Montessori educational philosophy. The staff takes pains to treat the kids with the respect and love which many of them do not receive at home.

Laura in action in the preschool room, Los Patojos

After the schoolwork is done, the staff often takes the kids on hikes outside the town. This in itself is bold. Hiking on the outskirts of the town is dangerous, not for the wild animals but for the wild humans one might *encounter. Though they have grown up in the neighborhood, the kids are not familiar with the paths. They are game for anything, but they are not hikers. After the first day when we North Americans gave away all our drinking water to the kids who had brought none, we volunteered to bring water along for everyone. The staff likes to have fun with the kids. On a particularly steep section, I told the kids around me to be careful with their feet, so they would not fall. At the same moment, the staff member said, "OK kids, RUN!" Parenting techniques are different in Guatemala.*

Juan Pablo, the founder, has a vision for social justice which pervades the center. He teaches the kids to be the leaders of tomorrow, to have an understanding of the political realities of Guatemala and abroad, and to have a sense that they can make a difference in the world. The staff gets together periodically to talk about political realities and how to create justice in Guatemala. This month, the teens are creating a newsletter, and they are planning an evening break dance event for the community—this in one of the most severely disadvantaged communities in the country, where people do not feel safe venturing out after dark.

The first day, I roamed around the center, getting to know the rhythms of the afternoon and exploring the activities offered to the various age groups. From teaching jump rope, beading and painting with the youngest ones, to reading a simple book and working out English words with the older ones, to just sitting quietly with a child as he did his homework, helping him or her to concentrate better in that wildly festive atmosphere, I felt needed and helpful right away. Within a few minutes, children started to approach me with questions. I felt a little hand on my shoulder, and a hesitant "Seño— puedes ayudarme?" "Teacher, can you help me?" At the end of the day, I was showered with hugs from many kids. Even more gratifying: when we walked through the neighborhood after the sessions, I met many of the parents, who greeted us with smiles of recognition. Numerous times, they came up to me to thank me for being there for their children.

One day, Juan Pablo told me that the oldest elementary-aged children, aged ten to twelve, needed some volunteer help. So I told Rafa, the coordinator of that group, that I was available to take a group. I had no idea what would happen a few minutes later when a dozen children assembled eagerly in their classroom, ready for what I had to offer. As it turned out, we had a wonderful conversation ranging from geography (Where is Kenya? What direction is the United States from here?) to how it feels to fall into a huge snow bank. I found that the children knew the Happy Birthday song in English but they did not know what the words meant. After we learned this we launched eagerly into the Spanish rejoinder, "Ya queremos pastel!" "We want cake now!" which they taught me. I look forward to an ongoing conversation with the group, helping them to discover their voices and learn more about the world and the role they can play to make it better.

Kids at Los Patojos (the mural reads "Without love, we are nothing")

Geography: I gave a lecture on the world map to the older children. It turns out they have very little understanding of geography. So I stood at the whiteboard and sketched the world map for them. We talked about the continents, the equator, and the oceans. We talked about the convention of putting north on top and south down below. Why? Because the map makers were from the north. We turned our heads upside down and tried to imagine what the map would look like with south on top. This exercise was uninteresting to them. First, because they do not know what the world map looks like. Second, because they are in the middle anyway.

This week, I will talk with them about Africa. When I asked some of them what is happening in northern Africa this year, most of them were unfamiliar with Mubarak's departure, or crises in Tunisia, Libya or elsewhere. One of them told me he had heard about Egypt, that it was the biggest empire on earth. I asked him where he had heard this. "In the Bible," he said.

A minor unpleasant incident: One day I bought a tiny beaded bag on a string in the market: a small trinket, useful for holding a single key or a bus token. It was bright blue. When I arrived at Los Patojos, all the girls loved it. One girl asked if she could wear it for a while and I readily consented. At the end of the day, when the kids had left, I realized that she had not returned it. This presented me with a conundrum. While I could easily write the item off as lost, or buy a new one for less than I would pay for a cup of coffee at home, I was concerned about the possible cultural implications. If I did nothing about it, would this be seen as a sign that it is acceptable to take items from foreign volunteers, inadvertently or not? Would the girl report to others that I had given her a gift, a valuable item in their peer group, and would it be thought that I was playing favorites? Would the incident affect the staff's intention to make the program a safe place for all, an ethical place where even minor theft is not tolerated? After some consideration, I mentioned it first thing the next day to Juan Pablo, the director, guessing that he had dealt with this issue before. To my relief, he handled it beautifully. He found the girl who had just arrived, and quietly asked her about the item. It turned out she had it in her pocket and returned it to me swiftly. Nothing more was said. I was impressed by the sensitivity of the staff, and their respect for boundaries while navigating a tricky cultural divide.

Buses – by Laura

I'm thinking about buses.
Here, they shake with color
And fill with music.

It doesn't come from the stereo,
But up from the ripped leather seats,
Whose broken metal frames like to sharpen their teeth on pant legs.

But never mind those ravenous monsters.
It comes from the cracked leather and chipped walls,
Bubbling past our ears and flowing through the windows,
Mingling with the clouds of exhaust we leave behind.

I think maybe that's what these people are made of,
That music and color that spills out of their buses,
Appears in a mango-colored window,
In so many woven art works
And skillfully mixed bowls of guacamole.

I enjoy the buses here -
These traveling fiestas on wheels.

Huipiles: *The indigenous women wear their traditional woven skirts and a matching hand-woven huipile blouse. The huipiles are a riot of color, yet each is carefully planned. Each village has its own style, and each blouse takes up to six months of full-time work to be embroidered by hand. Birds, flowers, stripes and zigzag patterns predominate in bold patterns, contrasting with the shy smiles on the women's faces as they greet us with a "Buenos días!" The women carry their goods to market balanced on their heads, wrapped in a large woven blanket. Usually there is a baby or small child peering out of the wrap that they carry across one shoulder. Despite their heavy burdens, they step lightly off the high curb and among the wind-strewn plastic bags on the street.*

Namaste: *Last week I was assigned to travel to a nearby village where all the women wore traditional woven clothing, including a woven skirt,* *a huipile, and the traditional wide sash. I learned that the sash is a great place to store your cell phone, and all the women had at least one. The work of these women was to make huipiles. We met in one of the women's homes, where we sat in a circle. Some of the older women did not read or speak Spanish, but they were respected as elders, with much wisdom to offer. To start the meeting, everyone brought their loan payments which were carefully recorded in the handwritten ledger books by the younger women, and receipts were given out. Then there was a discussion led by one of Namaste's traveling business advisors on how to set prices. Most of the women find that they cannot set a price high enough to compensate them for the time they have worked on their masterpieces. They complained that it takes several months' work to make a huipile, but the tourists will pay only $250, which works out to about 30 cents an hour.*

This week we went to another village and met with another group to offer education. Instead of sewing handicrafts, this group ran general stores, tortilla shops or flower shops. All the women had aprons over their modern clothing. These women were much less traditional than last week's group, and more outspoken. The laughter and sharing went on long after the formal session had ended. We talked about lots of things, like how to keep a customer waiting who comes in when it is busy (make eye contact with a smile!) and whether to allow customers to buy on credit. It was encouraging to see these women sharing information and suggestions with each other.

Work with Namaste is keeping me busy and feeling needed. It is challenging to see how marketing concepts can be made interesting and useful to women who are semi-literate. Most of them are naturally good business women and they understand the concepts right away, putting their issues into a larger context. I am organizing curricula for the program, using the tried-and-true marketing techniques of Product, Price, Promotion, Person (Customer) and Place. We had an interesting conversation about setting price based on the market demand instead of on the cost. Many of them do not have a clear sense of the cost of their product, so they tend to set prices based on "what the market will bear". This helps to move the product, but at the end of the week when they find out how little they have made, they may have to try selling something else.

A Namaste craftswoman at work on her handloom

The business advisors are from the same culture as the business owners, which is a great advantage. They have been small business owners themselves, and most of them have a knack for teaching. They bring out the shy participants and give each woman a chance to be in the "hot seat" for a few minutes during the discussion, so she can receive support and encouragement from the others.

I have been collecting data to help Namaste with their outcome measurements. For each household, we collect ten data points, ranging from whether the children are in school to whether the household owns a pig. Visiting the borrowers' homes, it is clear by observation whether they have a refrigerator and whether the floor is dirt or cement. We don't need to ask the question, but can simply gather the data during our informal discussion. On the other hand, one of the measures in the survey questions whether the household has a grinding stone for corn. The family may own a grinding stone, but not use it, if they have enough cash to go to the neighborhood mill instead. In the more urban villages, they may buy cornmeal or even prepared tortillas. These issues make the survey more challenging than it appears. One has to have faith in the survey instrument to gather data which do not seem to have an impact on the result, economic status.

Answers to the ten questions create a score for the household that correlates well in studies worldwide with the family's percentage likelihood of living under the poverty level. The scores do have validity at the group level. Namaste will conduct surveys at intervals with the same groups, before and after their loans have been repaid, to determine whether the households as a group are better off after their loans than they were beforehand. Outcome measurement is more and more important to donors, for good reason. Is our work making a difference? Do people have more disposable income and better health after they have been working with us? Are their children more likely to be in school? This Grameen technique is a simple tool that has shown promise to measure the outcome of anti-poverty programs throughout the world.

Second hand clothing: *We passed a man wearing a sweatshirt from Berwick Academy. I had to bite my tongue not to blurt out, "Hey! I've heard of Berwick! Have you actually been to Maine?" On second thought, which happily happened soon after the first one, I realized that the man has no connection to our friends at home. Instead, he purchased the sweatshirt in a used clothing market. In these markets, usually on the outskirts of cities, clothing comes in from the United States by the ton and is sorted and re-sold in an entirely different context from its original use. Shirts with writing in English are desirable, and we saw some men wearing shirts that announced, "Girl Power!" or "2004 National Cheerleading Competition". If these macho guys knew what they were wearing, they would be mortified.*

Eventually I get used to the idea that people do not know the meaning of the slogans on the cast-off clothes they are wearing. Or rather, the clothes have their own new value system, one that is recognized by the buyers, sellers and current owners of the clothes. I do not know these subtle distinctions in value, just as I do not understand some of the colorful Guatemaltecan expressions that still shoot right over my head.

Complaints: *Last night, I started with a perfectly good dinner idea and ruined it. I hastily put way too many chili peppers in the beans. Then try as I might, I couldn't fix the dinner. I added potatoes and pasta to soak up the spice. I even went out to the store to buy more beans in a desperate attempt to salvage the dinner. When I was at the store, the kids didn't tend the beans, and they burned. It was a complete disaster. The kids were very brave and tried to eat it, but even Evan who usually puts away a mountain of food professed not to be hungry.*

The worst thing was that I didn't really apologize. I blamed the chilies, and blamed in my mind the kids who let it burn. The saving grace of the meal was the three big heart-shaped chocolate brownies I gave them to thank them for being wonderful kids—my Valentine's Day gift to them on a special day. However, they didn't like them: too cakey. So it was a dinner from hell.

I tend to be too busy. Even on my sabbatical year, I'm filling up my time with lots of volunteer work, being the ongoing travel agent for the family, and providing three square meals a day. So yesterday I spent the day reading a novel. And then today I made the dinner again.

I wonder whether the kids could or should do more to help lead us on this trip. The model we are following is very old-school, very Mommy-knows-best. Before we left, they did not have much time to help with the planning. And now they are very happy to follow along with the plans I have made. I ask them all the time if they would like to do something differently, to move to a different country or city, and they decline. So we keep on with what seems to be working, and I continue to be in charge, like it or not.

Our neighbor's altar: *Our neighbor found a plywood board that has figures on it. He first saw the open Bible, then the Virgin, then Christ on* *the cross. Angels with wings could be seen around the edges, then more and more Bibles, crosses, and saints. A cynic might say that the forms are chance occurrences caused by the colors and shapes making up the board. The local priest says it is a miracle. Our neighbor has converted his garage into a sanctuary, and a weekly service is held in front of the board. There are always fresh flowers in the sanctuary. Often when I come home, my neighbor is praying there alone. He has plenty to pray about. His brother was killed in a random shooting, leaving him with a sister-in-law and her three children as family.*

__Building Stoves in Xela:__ We just came back from a long car ride to Xela, the place of ten peaks, otherwise known as Quetzaltenango, the place of the quetzal bird. The bird is no longer there, having left this sprawling metropolis in search of greener hills.

Xela is filled with unremarkable streets and small storefronts, an elegant central park and a museum whose wooden floorboards recall the old shops of my childhood, with their faded blue paint. The first floor contains a touching history of technology, from the town's first telephone bank, to mimeograph machines and the first portable telephones. Another room is devoted to the proud history of Xela, once the capital of its own separate country in Guatemala's western region. In the 1920s it was a modern city of coffee barons and had a working railroad system. A third room is filled with natural history oddities, from a family of stuffed lions with outsized staring marble eyes and ragged fur to jars of sad white fetuses, some human and some animal. Hanging in midair is a stuffed goat with eight legs splayed in all directions. It is said to have lived for several hours and gave off a strange yellow smoke when it breathed. One imagines the schoolchildren crowding around to read the descriptions and the undercurrent of Satanic urges hinted at by the commentary.

Our purpose in visiting Xela was to help to build fuel-efficient stoves that have chimneys, helping to avoid respiratory disease, the leading cause of death among children in Guatemala. We met our friends in the early morning and took the city bus out to a nearby suburb. It is a place of dusty brown hills on the edge of a mine, where trucks lumber in and out all day long, spewing exhaust. The homes are simple, with tin roofs and dry, rocky yards. Now is the dry season between the harvest and the next season's rains, and the land looks especially bereft. Instead of crops, the little tracts hold broken buckets and discarded plastic sandals.

Children helping us build a stove in Xela

The children crowded around as we worked, and helped wherever they could. The kitchen was a small room with a dirt floor, attached to the main house and sided in tin. The mother dug an expert hole, working in her sandals, while the children hauled firewood and furniture out of the kitchen to make way for their new stove. After a morning's work, we left our new concrete and cinderblock frame to dry. On a later trip, volunteers will put in the firebox and install the shining metal cook top and chimney. The family will no longer have to cook over a simple fire in the kitchen building or breathe in the smoke.

A trip to Comalapa: Another weekend, we took a bus trip to Comalapa, a town in the Western Highlands. It is known for its artwork, and recently, for a small non-profit organization started by a friend in Massachusetts. The organization is called Long Way Home. Its mission is to build sustainable schools using alternative and mainly recycled materials, and to be a demonstration site for both carbon-neutral operations and for innovative education. The first school is under construction; it is a place full of optimism, with composting toilets and the only playground in town.

The Sunday market in Chichi: Sunday is the big market day in Chichicastenango. The market stalls fill up the streets, leaving only a narrow corridor for customers to walk. Textile sellers marketing mainly to tourists are in abundance, along with those targeting the local market, who sell the ubiquitous used clothing, pots and pans, electronics, fragrant tropical fruits and everything else imaginable. There is an indoors commercial center packed with fruit and vegetable sellers. We went upstairs and looked down on the crowd, a riot of colors and activity. In this strongly Mayan part of Guatemala, almost all the women and some of the men wear brilliant homemade woven clothing. The designs are gorgeous.

What I notice most about people in rural Guatemala is that they seem to be always carrying heavy things. The girls are trained from an early age: girls as young as eight carry their younger siblings on their backs; they carry firewood with forehead straps; they help their mothers to cart merchandise to market and set it up. Boys probably work too, but it is the sight of so many little girls carrying burdens that look as heavy as they are that I notice most. One rarely sees that in the United States, in any cultural group. Men also carry preposterously heavy loads, when they are working: men in the marketplace sometimes carry three huge crates of fruit, towering over their heads. In general people in the villages are the beasts of burden; we did not see any donkeys or horses sharing the load.

Knives for sale in the market are shaped like guns, like killing instruments. They are hard to look at given the news that shouts out from the newspaper each day: a nurse killed on her way home from work, stuffed into a car trunk. She merits a short paragraph, with not even any speculation about the killer, his motivation, or any murder investigation. Guatemala may be one of the most beautiful countries in the world, yet it is also tragically one of the most violent.

The Interamerican Highway: *On the way back from Chichi, we spent a long dusty afternoon heading south and east back to Antigua by bus. We took the main road, the highway of Guatemala. Its dusty margins were covered by a perpetual fog of exhaust fumes, in which sat sellers with their tropical fruits:* mamays, *huge as a monkey's head, hiding a clear yellow freshness inside, and* sapotes *with their dented, rotted appearance from the outside and the orange fruit like sweet squash. Another fruit looks like a large plum, with a shocking neon purple flesh surrounding small black seeds. Even pineapples here look exotic. Picked ripe instead of green, each fruit is alive with color from pale green to bright yellow, advertising its exquisite sweetness.*

The road is called the Interamerican Highway, the main conduit for traffic of all types from El Salvador and parts south on up to Mexico and the United States. Travel on the highway is slow. Here the mudslide of last year came pouring over the bridge, the bridge still under repair and cars crawling around it through the underbrush. There a fuel truck has turned over on its side, and its driver has come back to alert the travelers to slow to a single lane. The sight of it lying on its side like a dead animal was somehow shocking, its fuel tank miraculously intact. Once we were jolted by a car coming towards us at full tilt, a construction detour unannounced to travelers coming from our direction. Another time, an eighteen-wheeler turned sharply on the mountain road and became completely wedged across the highway, stopping traffic in both directions for an hour. Finally, skillful driving allowed it to be cleared. I was glad we were not on the way to the airport that day. These experiences provided an instructive lesson on why it is impossible to get anywhere on time in the developing world.

We saw pickup trucks coming south with California license plates carrying loads of new items: car bumpers, washing machines, new bed frames. We saw white panel trucks driving north with no company name, shut tight. One can imagine so many refugees packed tight inside, sweltering in the heat and praying for a safe journey. One day this violence reached its tendrils into my life as well, when someone took the numbers of my debit card and security code from the automatic teller machine I used. The numbers made their way down this highway to Bogota, Columbia. There, some desperate person turned those magic numbers into cash, a small tax on the rich for use by those in need. I did not even have to bear the cost, due to the safety net of the United States banking system which reimbursed my loss. When the same thing happened to my Guatemalan friend, he lost $800, which was an absolute fortune to him. His bank ignored and perhaps even smiled on the theft. There is talk that these thefts are orchestrated from inside the bank.

Lago Atitlán: When I say we were never robbed on our trip, I don't mean we were not ever taken advantage of. Rip-offs are most common in tourist areas, where it is seen as a fair game to separate the tourist from some of his cash. We spent a night on the lovely Lake Atitlán, where many North American expats go to abandon the rat race altogether and make a new life selling trinkets or flipping tortillas on the street. The area attracts tourists like a magnet: a beautiful lake surrounded by dramatic mountains and picturesque Mayan villages. One weekend, we took a boat across the lake to a quiet village for a bit of relaxation. As a rare splurge, we stayed in a hotel for the night, swam in the lake and ate a good meal. The only problem occurred when we awaited our boat trip back, at dawn the next day. We had paid a good portion of the return fare, but not all of it, to encourage the motor boat driver to return for us as he had promised. But apparently we had paid too much of the return fare, with the result that he did not care to show up for the rest, and we had to find a different way to get across the lake. It was difficult to relax and enjoy the experience of dawn on the lake, when we knew we might miss our bus back to Antigua. But Conor made the most of it and wrote this poem:

Dawn on the Lake – by Conor

The fog rising from the expansive lake creates a blanket
Covering the view of the towering volcano.

The early morning sun is just starting to
Creep out from its bed and climb over the mountains.
The birds swoop silently in and out
Of the clouds like mosquitoes on a cool fresh summer's night.
Their reflections zip back and forth
On the top of the water.

Unbroken silence is denied by the small waves rhythmically lapping
Against the dock.
The sounds drifting over from the nearby town are
Barely audible.
Cars driving on the road seem timid,
Not fully awake yet.

In the middle of the lake, three centuries away,
A figure
Resembling the ferryman across the River Styx
Slowly paddles his way across the lake.
Shrouded in a cloak of mist and fog,
Solemnly gliding across the water.

Once he reaches the shore, he mutely passes the
Long row of women doubled over rocks in the shallows,
Painstakingly scrubbing dirt out of their clothes.

An ocean away, as if underwater, a horn
Signals the farewell of the early boat
Leaving,
Leaving this small town wedged in between the lofty volcano, the
shimmering lake, and the endless mountains.
Leaving,
Leaving,
Leaving,
Leaving
Leaving

Gone

QUAKER VOLUNTEER
WORK IN BOLIVIA

At the time of the spring solstice we flew south to autumn. In the southern hemisphere it was cold and rainy, with mountain air catching in our throats. We lived in the Cordillera Real, one of the highest mountain ranges in the world, as the fall weather progressed into winter. Our quest for endless autumn continued.

Sometimes a place is so foreign that you just stop short and take it in. You can't make any sense of it. You just let the reality wash over you. You look and listen, and experience. Bolivia was like that for our family. In many ways it was not easy. Mud was pervasive, food was sometimes limited, and despite the damp weather, there was no heat in the houses. Poverty in Bolivia is widespread, and it stares you in the face. We lived as the locals do, and so we experienced life as locals for a short while, though living in poverty doesn't count when you know that you will return to a life of relative luxury at home.

Bolivia was also where we worked the hardest. Having become proficient in Spanish, we were asked to teach English to high school students at two different schools, a public school and a parochial school. In the public school, the level was basic. English lessons were given in Spanish. In both schools the students needed clear explanations in Spanish before they were ready for our basic exercises and games. English had to be introduced patiently and slowly.

My children experienced their final exams of the Big Trip year in the Bolivian schools: teaching English to students older than they, with most of the teaching conducted in Spanish. Coming at the end of the year, it tested their verbal and persuasive abilities as well as their knowledge of Spanish and English grammar.

Conversation as a means to language learning was a new idea to the students. We started at a basic level. The children and I taught as teams, in one or two classrooms at a time. We gave the children sample scripts, which we wrote on the board. "How many brothers do you have?" "I have three brothers." We each went up and down the rows of students, explaining the exercise and helping pairs of students or small groups to interact with each other in order to practice their language skills.

Books were at a premium. In the public school, the only English books were donated and full of errors. Starting on the first page, we tried to correct "aple" and other similar mistakes. We soon found that the task was nearly impossible. A more successful venture was to find mp3 lessons online and download them to the school's computer lab. All the students had cell phones that would play mp3 files so we used this resource, encouraging them to download English lessons which we had transcribed. What they needed most was to practice listening, speaking and understanding basic dialogues. All of these tasks were totally foreign to the teacher, whose teaching skills and knowledge of English were minimal.

In the parochial school, there were good books, grammatically correct but in many cases culturally inappropriate. When the teachers assigned us to teach a lesson that asked the students to describe taking a plane ride to visit their grandmother, they all drew a blank, since none of them had ever ridden in an airplane. So we suggested a more appropriate lesson. In both schools, the teachers on the whole were dedicated to their work, and like most teachers everywhere, they were overworked and underpaid.

Martha's fan club at the parochial school

We divided our time between a mountain town called Sorata and the capital, La Paz. We taught English in both places. We lived first in Sorata, where it is easier to breathe. La Paz is the highest commercial airport in the world, at thirteen thousand feet elevation. Arriving from the Guatemalan highlands at five thousand feet, we were immediately aware of the need to go to lower ground. Sorata is at a much more tolerable eighty-eight hundred feet. Further, it is a lovely small town, nestled into the high mountains. It serves as a base for many tourists interested in the extreme sports available on the Cordillera mountain range.

Sorata is also the location of a wonderful Quaker education program run by the Bolivian Quaker Education Fund, or BQEF. Quakers connected with BQEF started a student residence, or *Hogar Estudiantil,* to house indigenous students from the Aymara culture who live far outside town. Most of the students live in remote mountain villages with no high schools. As a result, those who wanted to attend school had been renting rooms independently in Sorata if their families could afford it, not a safe plan for a rural high school student, especially for girls. Unfortunately, Bolivia has extremely high rates of rape and domestic violence, according to the United Nations Fund for Gender Equality. Because of the Hogar, the students are able to attend high school, and are often the first generation to gain a high school degree. I was familiar with the work done in the Hogar prior to the Big Trip, through some grant writing assistance I had provided. It is a remarkable program. In addition to its operation of the Hogar, BQEF provides a number of other educational programs, including college scholarships to fifty students in La Paz.

In Sorata, we lived in the guest room at the Hogar, where we were welcomed into the student community from morning to night. We accompanied the students to school and taught most of them English over the course of the day. In the afternoons we participated in their enrichment programs, working at their organic farm and playing sports with the students. Evan had brought silk-screening supplies and enough t-shirts for each of the Hogar students to make his or her own shirt. This learning turned into a micro-entrepreneurship venture, with students designing, producing and selling t-shirts to support their programs. In short, we became friends, teachers and advisors in our time in Sorata.

Sorata is three hours away from La Paz by public microbus. Even as we became accustomed to the higher elevation of the Andes, travel to La Paz made our heads and eyes ache. Chewing on (legal) coca leaves that could be purchased in any market by the bundle was the best antidote by far, and over the course of several weeks our altitude symptoms eased. We traveled to La Paz each weekend; eventually we moved there for several weeks of teaching. During that time, we rented a couple of rooms from a wonderful family who hosts international volunteers. On weekends we explored other areas of the country, traveling on public buses.

A student with her silk-screening creation

Not many people eat out in restaurants in Sorata, aside from the few foreigners who frequent a couple of pizza joints priced for tourists. There are a few market stalls that sell *api*, a warm pink drink whose ingredients seemed rather mysterious. It is a bracing concoction made from ground purple corn and sugar, excellent for early mornings in the cold mountain air. Sometimes we bought meat pies on the street, and occasionally we ate out at one of the few Bolivian restaurants in town that served Bolivian food. A major item on the menu, and one that we found very sustaining, was the *choclo*, or corn, that is served on the cob throughout the Andes. Quite the opposite from our tender kernels, eating choclo felt like eating cow corn. It was a meal in itself, with a hearty flavor and little sweetness—but sustaining. Choclo, api and quinoa are among the ancient Andean foods that have been passed down through the centuries, part of a cultural wisdom that is still very much alive. However, due to the high poverty level in Bolivia, malnutrition is high and life expectancy is the lowest on the continent. The price of food is increasing rapidly and many people do not get enough to eat.

As we found everywhere we travelled, it helped to have contacts in Bolivia. We came to Bolivia as volunteers working with BQEF. Though we located our own housing in La Paz, our Quaker friends welcomed us and helped us immeasurably along the way. They placed us in schools that needed our assistance, and they provided advice and an instant sense of community. We visited a different Quaker church each weekend under their care, learning about their interpretation of Quaker faith and values. As evangelical Friends, they practice their faith in a different way from ours, but we share the Quaker testimonies of non-violence, integrity, equality and simplicity. The web of worldwide community formed our major support system.

From my journal:

Arrival in Bolivia: When we arrived in La Paz, our main concern was the altitude. We had been told to gather our suitcases, drink some coca tea in the airport (it is a legal drink here, an infusion of the coca leaf from which cocaine is made), and head to a lower altitude with all due haste. In fact, it didn't take long for me to feel light-headed and a bit queasy, even sitting in the airport. I think we lost some of our powers of concentration, because it took us three hours to fill out the entry paperwork, change money, buy a SIM card for the phone, drink our tea and then get on the road downhill. I don't remember much about the trip since I lay down in the back seat and slept during the trip, catching glimpses of enormous snow-covered mountains when I was able to open my eyes.

In Sorata, we spent the better part of the next day fast asleep. When we awoke, we found ourselves in a pretty little town set in the midst of huge green mountains on all sides and dominated by the snow-capped Illampu, one of Bolivia's highest peaks. Sorata is in the foothills of the Cordillera

Real (or Royal Range) and there is little through traffic on the dirt road that passes for the main highway. You don't think about motors much until you don't hear them. It is so quiet here that we can hear the river a mile away, roaring down through the rocky valley.

The students living in the Hogar generally go home to their families' farms on weekends. Every Friday afternoon they head out on foot in different directions, some walking five or six hours on mountain paths to get home for the weekend. When I asked one young student where she lived, she said to me, "See that farthest peak? I live there." And off she went, with her long velour skirt, her many petticoats and her long braids. She would get there long after dark.

Living in the southern hemisphere: *I have apparently internalized on a deep level my life as a northerner. Here in the southern hemisphere during the day, the sun appears to be in the wrong place. When the sun is on my right, I am traveling west. This feels very strange. What is the sun doing over there in the northern half of the sky?*

Teaching: *In the private school, we were asked to teach using religious songs. We were stumped as to songs that would provide an easy English vocabulary, until we thought of spirituals. Some of the songs were challenging to explain and we decided to act them out. In teaching "Swing Low, Sweet Chariot", we ran into a snag trying to explain the third verse: "If you get to heaven before I do, drill a hole and pull me through." At this point in the song, one of us climbed up on a chair, pantomiming a drill and pretending to pull another of us up. The students looked puzzled even after the jokes and explanations. The theological ramifications of that verse are a bit confusing, even though we have been singing it forever. We may have created our own cultural confusion with that one.*

Día del Mar: *One of the saddest days of the year in Bolivia is the Día del Mar, the day of the sea. Bolivia has no seacoast, having lost access to a route to the Pacific in a war with Chile and Peru that ended in 1883. Bolivians feel that their economy is stunted by the lack of access to the ocean, a factor that has certainly had a huge impact on the economy. Paul Collier, in his book,* **The Bottom Billion,** *which analyzes patterns of poverty among the world's poorest inhabitants, posits the impact of a* country's being landlocked, along with civil war and tension with one's neighbors, as one of the main risk factors for losing the fight for economic progress.

So on the Día del Mar, Bolivians pay homage to the sad fact that they have no seacoast. For weeks prior to this event, students formed marching bands and parades and practiced in the streets. On the day itself, everyone turned out for a community-wide performance in front of the town hall in Sorata. Students read poems lamenting the loss of the seacoast, politicians made speeches, banners were displayed and musical parades went on for most of the day. One could not help but be affected by the whole society's yearning. It was a sad day.

Playing ultimate Frisbee with cows: We had brought a number of Frisbees with us on the Big Trip to give away, along with basic Frisbee throwing lessons. In Sorata, there were enough young people to make a proper Ultimate Frisbee team, and land to play on. But there were no athletic fields, just a large meadow that was somewhat boggy underfoot. The biggest problem was the cows. There were several cows grazing and though we periodically tried to herd them into a corner of the field, they quickly moved back out to the middle where we were trying to play. Avoiding the cow plops and the mud was one thing. The kids had the added challenge of avoiding cows while running for a pass or throwing the Frisbee. Luckily, there were no violent encounters between human and beast.

Playing Frisbee in a cow field

A bright green memory: Sitting in the late afternoon in the student residence in Sorata, Bolivia. After a long morning of teaching, then walking home on a muddy road, we all (students and visiting teachers alike) had lunch and then washed our muddy clothes. The girls washed some of their enormous skirts or polleras, *consisting of huge lengths of skirts and petticoats of about four yards each. When hung out to dry, they formed big smiles on the clothesline. The boys scrubbed their pants, socks and white sneakers. Later in the afternoon, as the rains cleared, some of us sat and played* samponas, *or Andean pipes, on the upstairs porch. The relaxation that comes from doing something on which you will not be tested, that is sheer fun and not required, fell on us all. The back porch sits at the top of the residence, like the prow of a ship looking out over the green hills on the opposite side of the valley. Sitting there was restful, with a view of the active courtyard, the river valley below, and the snow-capped peaks in the far distance. We were relieved to be relaxing, and relieved to have on fresh dry clothes that were not muddy. We sat together and chatted and joked. We made a community together.*

Guatemala and Bolivia: Coming directly from Guatemala, I am struck by the similarities—and the differences—between the two countries. Both have an indigenous majority, with a ladino *or Spanish-origin upper class. Both have huge disparities in income between rich and poor, placing among the top fifteen countries in the world on the Gini coefficient, a measure of income disparity. They both rank high on other measures of poverty as well. For example, fifty percent of children in Guatemala under five years old are chronically malnourished, the fourth highest rate in the world. Bolivia's rate is not much better, with thirty-seven percent in rural areas. Not surprisingly, these numbers have a racial dimension. While the poverty rate is declining in both countries, it remains stubbornly high among the indigenous, darker-skinned population. A World Bank report notes that in Bolivia and Guatemala almost three-quarters of the indigenous population is poor.*

Here in the Sorata highlands, 95 percent of the families experience nutritional challenges at various times of the year, especially in January before the harvest begins. There are no visible signs of malnutrition, though fruit and milk products seem to be luxuries not affordable to many. The price of quinoa, an excellent grain for its high protein and low fat qualities, has risen dramatically in recent years since the developed world has discovered it to be a good gluten-free source of protein. In the neighborhood, there is a lot of talk about the high price of food. Most children seem to attend school at least part time, though every morning I notice a number of school-aged children in town selling gelatin desserts to passersby.

Rural vendors in Sorata

Racism is rife in both countries, but in Bolivia, unlike in Guatemala, the top leadership is indigenous: Evo Morales is the first indigenous president in South America. He is not without his detractors, however, and Bolivia is a place where threats of violence stand in for political discussion. Peaceful negotiations have not worked in the past, and there is little faith that they will work now. Labor unions make huge demands for salary increases, and to underline their seriousness, protesters close off the streets and even set off dynamite to make craters in the pavement.

For example, this week in La Paz, workers have made a demand for a twenty percent increase in salaries for all government workers, responding to huge spikes in the price of natural gas, sugar and other necessities. Protesters have closed off the main highways. Protestors sit wall to wall in the streets surrounding the government buildings in La Paz. They share pots of food and play cards on the grass in the median strip, enjoying the sunny weather and their time off work. However, the demonstration is serious. We went over to have a look but we kept our distance, and turned back when we saw the riot police and demonstrators facing off in silent opposition. Now during the evening, we hear firecrackers and occasionally and more ominously, the sounds of dynamite further downtown.

After a few days, Evo met the protesters' demands in large measure, agreeing to an eleven percent increase in the public sector minimum wage. Will this huge increase be affordable to the Bolivian government, a tiny power on the world's stage?

In Guatemala there are no protests.

Another difference between Guatemala and Bolivia that we notice on a daily basis is the relative safety of daily life in Bolivia. Though there is a lot of petty theft as in any place where poverty is rampant, few weapons are in evidence. In Guatemala, we saw armed guards with semi-automatic rifles guarding company entrances, banks and even delivery trucks. To enter a bank you must be allowed in by an armed guard standing between two double locked doors. That is not the case in Bolivia. In Sorata, when a merchant leaves her store for a few minutes, she leaves the door open, placing a broom across the entrance to indicate her absence. That practice would have been unheard of in Guatemala. We can walk everywhere up in the mountains without worrying about safety from thieves. In Guatemala, tourists have been killed hiking up a nearby hill, within sight of town.

On a happier note, the food is entirely different here in Bolivia. We traveled from a warm climate with lots of local fruit to a higher, cooler climate in the Cordillera Real, the royal mountain range. So of course the food here is different, and much heartier. We are eating potatoes, wonderful vegetable soups, and bread, with few fruits.

Many families rely on farming in both places, since both countries have a rural population base. In both countries, and in fact, everywhere we have traveled, people often ask us, "What does your family farm?" I am embarrassed to admit that we "farm" some shrubs, a meager lawn, a perennial garden, and a few tomatoes and heads of lettuce that do not come near to sustaining us through the winter.

In Spain, they use the formal: Señor and Señora. In Guatemala they use the lovely Mi amor — *my love. "Which one would you like, mi amor? I offer good price for you!" In Bolivia, everyone is* amigo, *or friend. This word is used by everyone, in a rare show of egalitarianism.*

Exploring on foot, a novel concept: *Today was our day off. Our family went for a local hike and ended up quite lost down by the river, wandering around on little trails and retracing our steps for hours. We all enjoyed this aimless activity. Recreational walking has not yet taken hold in Bolivia. When we stopped to chat with an old woman on the road, she said, "Don't you have mobilidad?" It turns out that the word* mobilidad *in this region actually means a ride, a means of transport. Who would possibly not choose mobility over immobility, no ride? And what is wrong with these gringos who choose to walk along a muddy road when they can clearly afford to pay for the cheap buses that drive up and down at frequent intervals? It was beyond her that we would choose to walk around instead of riding.*

Even the concept of free time to take a hike was something she had probably never considered. The paths here are unlike those at home, where we find meandering paths made by teenagers looking for a view or a place to smoke, with lots of dead end paths. Here the paths all have a clear purpose: down to the river to wash clothes, up over the ridge and home out of town, or shortcuts that connect the road's endless zigzags. Not all paths are easy. We traversed some loose shale paths along the edge of the bank, with the river rushing cold and gray far below.

Life in La Paz: *La Paz is a very vibrant place. The streets are full of people and traffic at all hours. Sidewalk sellers display their wares across the entire sidewalk and out onto the streets. The lack of crosswalks and* *the extremely steep hills make for an energetic walking city. Many of the sidewalks are steep staircases. "Just pretend you're a car!" I said to Laura once as we wove among the buses circulating at full speed around a rotary. It's a good thing she is tall, taller than I. Microbuses are the means of transport for those without cars. They are privately owned and the competition is fierce. All you need is a bus not much bigger than a minivan, in which you can seat up to fifteen in a pinch, and a sign in the window indicating your route. Enormous numbers of people are transported very quickly this way, and there is rarely more than a few minutes' wait.*

There is so much activity on the street that it is hard to tell what is due to the protesters and what is normal background noise. I woke this morning to a Palm Sunday procession directly under my window, with hundreds of parishioners singing and waving palm branches in rhythm with a thirty-piece band. A few minutes later, I heard explosions downtown. It is all very mysterious.

Quaker gatherings: *Today was bookended by two very different religious celebrations. This morning we were invited to attend the 25th anniversary of a Quaker meeting in El Alto, the large indigenous community just above La Paz, on the Altiplano (high plain). It was quite cold in the church, but the crowd was energetic, and sang and prayed throughout a four-hour service. Laura and I represented the family, as the boys stayed home with stomach bugs. As is the usual practice, we were asked to come up to the microphone and make a presentation. This time we were specifically asked to offer a song that was quietly prayerful, not an alabanza, or praise song. We taught the community "Ubi Caritas", teaching it in Latin, English and Spanish. As always happens in these Quaker meetings, I felt the support and caring of the community hanging on our every word and gesture. Clearly, it means a lot to them to have foreign visitors. Afterwards we joined the congregation in an ample lunch of chicken soup and bread, and shared conversation with the women in their colorful wide skirts and bowler hats.*

Laura and Martha offering song and worship
at a Quaker celebration in El Alto

Tonight I wandered into the Quaker meeting house to hear a concert by a folk music group called Ministerio Canto Nuevo. The energy was electric as was the music, indigenous pipes and guitars amplified by a very modern sound system. The church was packed with families taking pictures with their cell phones of each other dancing to the music. Teens were up front, singing and clapping along, with a few young couples finding their own private rows to listen. Older people were clapping and swaying to the music, including one elderly blind man who kept time with his cane. The music was fabulous: traditional Andean music expressing the love of God. The musicians spoke of how hard the year has been, and how important it is to raise our voices and remember our joy.

The two celebrations were very different, but some of the same people were involved in both. The worship style of Quakers in Bolivia is very different from what we're accustomed to, and amplified Andean music is not what we usually hear when we go out in the evening. Yet I feel a connection with their worship and with their music. I sense how these practices feed their souls, and I feel comforted as well, welcomed into their community.

On meeting for worship among Santidad Friends: *I am surrounded by cries of repentance and whispered prayers. Most of the women have gone up to the altar to pray, where they kneel and sob their entreaties to God. Those who remain in the pews have turned around to kneel and place their heads on the seats, from where I hear tears and cries of anguish and repentance. The young girls near me are following their mothers' practice. A large number of the men have also gone to the altar, creating rows of kneeling petitioners two and three deep. The communal prayers have joined together into a sea of voices, so loud that the noises of the small children playing in the yard are hardly discernible. Towards the end of the prayer time, a woman stands and faces us, testifying with deep emotion to her past sins and her prayers for God's help.*

This worship service is entirely foreign to my family and me. We come from a "liberal Friends" tradition characterized by meetings for worship (not church services) that are not programmed. With neither minister nor planned program, our meetings are led by the inner Light inside each of us, leading to occasional spoken "ministry" offered out of the silence by participants.

I will never be a member of Santidad Friends, with their deep roots in the evangelical tradition. Yet when I go into their church, I enter a deep river of faith that washes their tradition and mine. I see their shared ministry, as various men and women take the microphone in the planned portion of the service. I hear their direct relationship with God as they pray, using the informal form of you:"Tu, Señor", and as they whisper their deepest fears and hopes. I appreciate their observance of the Quaker testimonies of peace, equality, integrity and simplicity, including the absence of jewelry worn on Sunday.

So as the prayer continues, I close my eyes and worship, tall (at least compared with my neighbors) and silent in my seat. I imagine below my feet a stream of energy connecting me to the rocky mountains in whose lap I sit, those mountains whose mines have brought grief and anguish, yet also economic survival, to many in this community. I imagine that my body has turned into a tree, whose green leafy branches extend above me. I have tuned into the vast positive energy of God's love. I feel this energy encircling us all and joining all beings everywhere, giving life force to the whole world. Earth's energy below connects to the energy of air above, the energy in which all living things grow and are bound together in a world of God's creation.

A conundrum: *A young woman student came to us and said she had been sexually assaulted. We advised her to go to the health center, but she was very timid and refused to go. Under questioning by her teachers, she recanted and denied that anything had taken place. What is the foreigner's role here? Should we ask questions and bring our cultural values to bear? Or should we keep quiet and let matters proceed as they would if we were not present? It's hard to tell what to do, and our hearts ache for her.*

Soccer Sunday: *Today we went to a soccer game with our host family here in La Paz. Their three boys love soccer, and we had a relaxing Sunday afternoon sitting at the field and watching them play. We had found out about Luis and Marta through chatting with the owner of a local handicraft shop, a woman with many connections to local service organizations. Luis and Marta welcome volunteers from the United States, Europe and Australia to share their home, paying rent by the week. We are invited to use the kitchen to prepare our own meals, though we often combine ingredients and eat together with our hosts and the other guests. I've learned some Bolivian recipes from Marta, and she has provided a friendly, open window on the lives of a middle-class, non-Quaker family.*

Machu Picchu and Potosí: *Recently we've taken two tourist trips that represent polar opposites in human existence. At the heights of Machu Picchu, we saw the impressive architectural, scientific and aesthetic accomplishments of the Inca civilization in fifteenth-century Peru. On the very top of the most inaccessible mountains, Incan engineers created huge stone dwellings, ceremonial spaces and terraced fields for livestock and agriculture. The city of Machu Picchu is perfectly located so as to maximize the northern sun. Part fortress, part city, access was controlled by the high mountain passes and intruders could be seen from far off. Would-be invaders had to travel the path in the hot sun, where their every movement would be observed by those in the city. Along the route, they had to pass through occasional guard houses where many soldiers could hide. The walkway is a good two meters wide, made of flat stones and steps that are still used to this day. Within the city, water channels brought clear running water underground into basins where jars could be filled, with benches for resting and observing the cool water. The channels still run clear today.*

Another amazing achievement of the Incas was their massive stonework. Towering walls twenty feet high are constructed of huge granite blocks, each weighing many tons. How did they hone these stones without power tools, so that they fit together tightly without a single chink? How did they raise them to form these imposing walls?

On the other end of the spectrum was Potosí. Currently the largest mining city in Bolivia, it was once the largest city in the entire Americas, with 800,000 inhabitants in 1574. In the seventeenth century, when New York was still Dutch, the Spanish ruled Potosí and worked the indigenous miners to death churning out silver and other minerals. These riches are on display in churches all over Spain. They are showcased most dramatically in Toledo and in the Escorial, the palace built by Phillip II as a monument to the Spanish monarchy. As we toured Potosí, I saw in my mind's eye the altarpieces and swords of Toledo and the royal mausoleums of the Escorial that we had visited just a few months previously.

Current day Potosí may be the saddest place I have ever visited. Worse even than the Lakota reservation in South Dakota, with its liquor stores just outside the reservation where non-natives prey on the locals. Potosí is garbage-strewn streets, where stray dogs and people wander at night in the cold wind to find a few items of value. Potosí is sixteenth-century Spanish buildings gone derelict with graffiti on their facades, and small children hawking polished stones in the central square. While the settlers in North America mainly killed the indigenous people they encountered, the Spanish settlers in Bolivia worked them to death, mining minerals to bring back to Spain. The suffering continues today.

The mine is still the biggest employer in town, and a mine tour is offered to tourists as a way to experience a small part of the horrific conditions that still reign there. We entered the mountain through a muddy hole no more than five feet high. As we were led into the depths of the mountain, we brushed against walls furry with asbestos, gleaming with bits of zinc and silver, and dripping with brown and yellow liquids. Occasionally we moved aside quickly as men came by us pushing wagons filled with stone, one ton each. Three men pushed and hauled each wagon along the track, uphill and down, to reach the mouth of the mine and dump it over the cliff onto the slag heap below. No mules or trucks are used inside the mine: men are the beasts of burden. To get through their day, they drink grain alcohol and chew enormous mouthfuls of coca leaves. The mountain is in imminent danger of collapse, having been drilled through for over four centuries. And yet men choose to enter the mines in order to survive, living for their dream of finding a large vein which will make them a fortune—or at least keep their families clothed and fed.

Potosí is the raw grinding of poverty against idle wealth and oppression. The whole city looks like a slag heap, with most items of value long since gone, whose citizens continue to look for a few crumbs. Over the centuries of the Spanish occupation of Bolivia, it is estimated that nine million Bolivians died in the mines, though no memorial has ever been built. The sadness of the past hangs over the present like a dense fog.

Workers dumping the slag outside the mine at Cerro Rico, Potosí

Song: Palm Sunday (Jesus of Potosí) by Evan

He pushes two tons of earth in a rusty cart—
The hill's meat forced out through its arteries,
And he picks away at its broken heart,
And breathes its dust working on his knees.

In these dark holes nine million died,
And a five-decade life is uncommon still;
Steeped in machismo and hard-won pride
He dies for the sins of our dollar bill.

To the capital with dynamite blasts,
So the last will be first and the first will be last,
With grain alcohol and coca leaves
In rides Jesus of Potosí.

It was once the world's greatest silver stash,

But Romulus and Remus sucked it dry.
Now he renders to Caesar Caesar's stolen cash
As martyrdom wages in a foreign buy.

To the capital with dynamite blasts,
So the last will be first and the first will be last,
With grain alcohol and coca leaves
In rides Jesus of Potosí.

The government square's blocked by police,
Roman Legionnaires in riot gear,
And though it's filled with charcoal doves of peace,
No olive branch will be found here.

To the capital with dynamite blasts,
So the last will be first and the first will be last,
With grain alcohol and coca leaves
In rides Jesus of Potosí.

Tourism that works: *We spent two nights on the shores of Lake Titicaca, a remote and mysterious-sounding place that straddles the borders of Bolivia and Peru. The lake is the site of the Inca creation story, and indeed it felt like the center of the earth. It is the highest navigable lake in the world, studded with round, treeless islands filled with terraced agricultural fields.*

We stayed with two different families, through carefully planned programs set up by the villagers to share the economic advantage that foreigners bring. Our first host family lived on a quiet peninsula reaching out into the enormous lake, with water and mountains on three sides. The second lived on the remote yet crowded island of Amantaní, which welcomes hordes of tourists every day, teaching them about its culture and profiting from the resulting economic benefit.

I'm glad we had the first night to ground us and to teach us how lovely this place is. We made our way to the village of Llachón via two buses and a half-hour walk on a dirt road to the very end of the peninsula.

We passed farmers, quiet thatched houses and sunny fields along the way. The landscape summoned up the rocky shores of coastal Maine, and the lives of our hosts were enviably simple, with hard work but seemingly enough of everything. Electricity and water were plentiful, and many homes sported solar panels which allowed them to take advantage of the bright sunny days. We helped our hostess to harvest oka, a potato-like tuber that features prominently in their diet. Small fish from the lake provided delicious protein for our meals, along with rice and vegetables. Their home was perched on the edge of the hill looking out over the lake, with sun-warmed rocks and a little green garden surrounded by flowers where the children's play awoke us in the morning. Our tiny room reminded me of Ireland, with its whitewashed walls and a small window decorated with geraniums. Four thick woolen blankets kept us warm through the cold night, but during the day we waded in the lake and we might have gone swimming.

Harvesting oka on Llachón peninsula

Traditional culture continues strong on the peninsula, with the Quechua language spoken by all, and home-spun fabrics with beautiful flower embroidery still worn by the women as daily clothing. Most surprising were the large four-cornered hats, with floral embroidery on top and two enormous pom-poms. The women wear these even while working in the fields. Our host family worked hard but their lives seemed to provide what they needed, in exquisite surroundings.

Our second home stay was on the island of Amantaní, a short boat-ride away from Llachón. When we arrived on Amantaní, we knew we were in for a different experience from that on the peninsula. Whereas we had arrived alone on the local bus at Llachón, we arrived at Amantaní along with a crowd of other tourists. As the boat pulled up to the dock, a large number of women in traditional garb, complete with white embroidered blouses, red skirts and black shawls, were waiting in a row to accept the foreign visitors into their homes. The boat captain efficiently assigned all the visitors to host families, and each group was led to a home on the hillside. After a good 20-minute scramble across the fields and over the stone walls, we arrived at our host family's home, a simple two-story structure with a cement courtyard in the center and several bedrooms upstairs and down. Each room was simply but adequately furnished with beds, many blankets, and an electric light bulb hanging from the ceiling.

After we settled in, it was suggested that we hike the central hill, called Pachamama, the Earth Goddess. When we arrived at the central plaza, we noted that all the visitors had been given exactly the same instructions, as we were joined by all our fellow boat-mates. We climbed the hill en masse to watch the sunset over the lake from this stunning setting. Towards the top, our family struck out for the neighboring hill, Pachatata, just to be different. We decided that Pachatata was slightly higher, and certainly quieter, than Pachamama with its large number of visitors and cameras whose flashes were visible from across the fields. The quiet breeze blowing through the grasses and the glorious sunset over the lake led us each to a quiet meditation of our own design.

Laura meditating at Pachatata

We came down in the dark, a companionable parade of travelers, to the central square where we met our host families to be escorted back to their homes for dinner. Our dinner was nutritious and ample, served in the kitchen and cooked over a three burner clay wood-burning stove. After dinner we were instructed to put on local clothing and go to a dance, where we again met our fellow travelers for an evening of beautiful Andean music and awkward dancing by groups of visitors wearing altogether too many layers. We had bundled against the cold prior to putting on the thick woolen skirts, ponchos and hats provided by our hosts, expecting an outdoors affair. We hadn't imagined that we would be in an indoors heated community center. I found it more enjoyable to sit and listen to the excellent music.

As we pulled away from the dock the next day, I reflected on what a great program the islanders had set up for their economic benefit while giving visitors a feeling for their way of life. The program of taking turns hosting visitors provides a huge economic boost to the isolated island and also allows them to maintain their traditions. The island community has worked out a system whereby the ten villages take turns, with each village hosting tourists three times per month, so that they are not overtaxed. The evening dances provide enjoyment for the locals as they visit, enjoy their own music, and poke lighthearted fun at the tourists dancing around in traditional clothing and foreign hiking boots. We decided that our hometown in New England, which lacks a large hotel, would do well to institute a similar program.

Conor's reflections on Peru:

We visited Peru on one of our vacations from volunteering in the schools in Bolivia. The food in Peru was delicious, and we bought gourmet foods for a third of the price we would get in the United States, as the Peruvian Sol is three to one dollar. A few of the specialties in Peru are llama, alpaca and guinea pig (known as cuy). Some restaurants serve the cuy standing up on a pizza, with his little claws intact. Llama and alpaca we did get to try, but we were eluded by the guinea pig. In my opinion, llama and alpaca taste the same, and they both mostly taste like beef.

Environmental efforts in Bolivia: Bolivia has just passed a very encouraging—and groundbreaking—law of protection for Mother Earth, or Pachamama, the earth goddess and creator of all in the indigenous Aymara tradition. The law reserves these rights: the right to life and to existence; to be respected; to regeneration of its biocapacity and continuance of its cycles and vital processes. Now lawsuits can be brought claiming damages to Pachamama.

Bolivia has been a leader internationally on environmental issues, encouraging the developed countries to pay to clean up the environment, and drawing connections clearly between poverty in the global south and climate change, caused mainly by the developed countries. The Andean population is entirely dependent on shrinking glaciers for their drinking water. The progressive philosophy of the Morales government plays a role in this debate, offering a strong presence at the United Nations with speeches calling for "Living Well" as a cultural alternative to capitalism.

Environmental awareness in Bolivia is strong, but the budget is not sufficient to the task, and enforcement will be hard to obtain. For instance, there are no laws in Bolivia against dumping trash on land or water. Just below our home in La Paz is a dirty river called Choqueyapu which is officially dead. Apparently 200,000 gallons of urine are dumped into it annually, along with tons of toxic waste from factories. The stench is noticeable as we walk to the bus stop beside its foamy chocolate-colored waters. There are no leash laws, and dodging dog excrement, which adds to the runoff, is a big part of walking around town. One day we saw some girls leaving an automotive business with a huge bucket which they dumped into the rushing waters without a care. As in most developing countries, environmental education and efforts take a backseat to the economic concerns of daily life.

On the other hand, the carbon footprint of most Bolivians is tiny. Imagine the impact of not heating your home, using mostly cold tap water with just a small electric heater for shower water, washing and drying your laundry by hand, and taking public transportation everywhere. So it appears that in most parts of the world the pollution is right under our feet, whereas in the so-called developed world, we create our pollution miles away from where we live, in our coal mines, our jet streams and our meat factories.

Economic Essay by Conor

"Do not worry sir, these are [dirhams, quetzals, shillings, or bolivianos], not dollars." We have heard this throughout our trip from desperate shopkeepers in markets. This cry seems to mean that since the price is stated in dirhams (Morocco), quetzals (Guatemala), shillings (Kenya), or bolivianos (Bolivia), it is somehow lower than it would be in dollars. The topic of economics in relation to travel is an interesting one. Seven or eight years ago, our family went to Canada in the winter and stayed at a fancy hotel, with a double floored-suite. I, being seven years old, wondered how we were able to do this. The answer was that the US dollar was much stronger than the Canadian dollar. On the other hand, while we were in Europe this past fall, the Euro was much higher than the dollar. Because of this, we ate mostly bread and cheese whenever we could.

Here in Bolivia, things are very cheap to us. For instance, in the small town of Sorata, you can buy five bread rolls for fifty cents and a Popsicle for twenty cents. We have been thinking a lot about why the price is so low, or at least seems that way to us. While hiking in the beautiful mountains surrounding Sorata, we had a conversation about this, and one conclusion we came to was how lucky we are to have been born in the United States. If we had been born in Bolivia, and had done the same job, we would have made bolivianos instead of dollars. As a result, things would seem seven times as expensive in the United States.

Taking an example like Popsicles, it led us to ponder why the price stays so low. The store owner seems to be the only ice cream seller in town, conveniently located on the main plaza, and he could set the price as high as he wants. However, he has to keep it low, because there's a point at which the market won't be able to bear the set price. Another possible reason that popsicles are relatively cheap in Sorata is that the cost of producing the Popsicle is less than in the United States. If the factory workers are getting paid less for making the Popsicle, the end product will cost less. The transportation costs of driving the ice cream into the mountains and keeping it cold are also less. This is because the gas price per gallon here is a little less than two dollars per gallon, much lower than at home.

Inflation is also a factor in the price differences. For instance, if a fruit seller thinks his mangoes will be more valuable tomorrow for whatever reason, he will charge more today. Other fruit sellers will then think that that is the accepted price for mangoes, and they will raise their price as well. After this spiral, someone from another country can come in and buy some things with their currency, which would be much stronger than that of the local currency. This is happening right now in Bolivia, where the prices of sugar and fuel are going up very fast. Even though the price might be too high for locals, things appear cheap to outsiders. That is what we experienced in Sorata buying Popsicles.

Trek above Sorata: *This was to be our big trekking weekend. We had purchased food and contracted for two mules to carry* la cocina—*the kitchen (as they call the stove, pans and equipment), food for six, tents and sleep gear up into the mountains. Eusebio, our host, who also has many* *years of guide experience, was to be our guide. Unfortunately, our hopes were dashed by a thick fog that enveloped us as soon as we got up into the hills. A slow rain started, and did not stop for our entire visit. We measured our hike in "Mount Washingtons", the 4000 feet change in elevation from where we usually park at Pinkham Notch in New Hampshire to the summit of Mount Washington, one of our favorite hikes.*

Mount Illampu from Sorata, on a sunny day

The first day we hiked up 4000 feet, or one Mount Washington. We camped next to a little lake in a saddle below the snowy summit of Mount Illampu. Arriving there felt just like arriving at the Lake of the Clouds, near the summit of Mount Washington, but without the hut to look forward to. The wind and driving rain made us eager to set up our tents and get into our sleeping bags, though it was only three in the afternoon. Once there, however, we discovered the limitations to our locally rented equipment. Tents and sleeping bags with no working zippers made it hard to keep warm, never mind staying out of the way of the rivulets of water that soon invaded the sides of the tent. We put on all our clothes and whiled away the afternoon reading The Little Prince *in Spanish.*

After a short supper in the rain, we went back to bed for a long night of practicing sleeping. Laura and I got to laughing, since the lack of oxygen made us sound like two dogs panting in the hot sun. It is hard to fall asleep when you're breathing as if you are walking uphill. We spent the night listening to the rain on the roof of the tent and wondering if the weather would ever clear up.

Unfortunately the morning brought more of the same: pea soup fog, with a possibility of snow above us. We decided to head back down to Sorata. Unfortunately, we were never able to see across the lake from our campsite, which supposedly has an odd configuration of colored rocks that look like eyes, making eerie faces when the lake and its reflection in the water are seen sideways. We never did hike the second Mount Washington, our destination at the glacier's base, located at fifteen thousand feet elevation. We may have had problems breathing up there anyway. What we did see—a beautiful, quiet subalpine wilderness—made us glad to have made the trip as far as we did.

Where meat comes from: *I saw an article on meat eating in the US press, and the topic seemed far away from our experience living in the global south. The article was about how to make consumption of meat seem more real, to appreciate the animals that died, whether to eat meat at all, and the like. Here in Bolivia we see death every day. A regular sight in the streets is a wheelbarrow filled with meat parts, for example, a cow's head with some fur still attached, the eye gazing out at us from a skinned face.*

Laura and I went for a run and there was a dead dog in the middle of the road, his muzzle frozen in death's agony. We see exactly what happened, that the dog is not really here anymore. The dog's expression gives some sense of how it felt. When people in the developing world get meat, they are thankful for having it. It is expensive. The prize for the youth soccer tournament was a sheep. It cost a great deal, they said: the price worked out to thirty-five dollars. The winning team would take it home, kill it and appreciate its meat. All the teens here know how to butcher a large animal.

When you can gain access to meat, it keeps hunger away effectively. I am reminded of the Kenyan dish made with kale: sukumawiki. The direct translation is "stretches the week". When you don't have enough money for meat, sukumawiki staves off hunger for a bit and keeps you strong. Here in the Bolivian highlands, the diet is composed mainly of meat and potatoes. In this cold climate, protein and starch are the means of survival.

All this is not to suggest that we all cart around wheelbarrows full of cow parts. Just to note that a concern for whether we are experiencing the "reality" of our food comes from our very privileged experience of the world. We do not have to do any of the messy work of raising, killing or preparing our food. Our wealth has allowed us to step away from this work and yet to keep all the benefits of plentiful, cheap food. Perhaps from time to time we should at least notice how other people live so we don't forget where our meat comes from.

Where cocaine comes from: It comes from the foothills of the Andean range in South America, including here in Bolivia. Among the many points of conflict between the United States and the Bolivian government is an argument about production of coca, the base element of cocaine. Coca leaf is legal here and is a staple in the Bolivian diet, used as a mate (tea) or chewed. It is a stimulant that reduces hunger and also relieves soroche, the altitude sickness that comes from the dramatic changes in altitude involved in travel in the Bolivian highlands. For example, the bus trip from here in Sorata to central La Paz which many take weekly, involves a climb from 8,800 feet to 12,000 feet. Even today, miners rely on coca leaf to travel many feet below ground level and work for long hours without *enough food. Coca consumption is a part of the Bolivian culture. It also has a strong ceremonial aspect and is considered to facilitate insights from the spiritual world during meditation.*

The Bolivian government has determined the amount of coca that is used for internal consumption and is working to keep production low enough to meet those legitimate uses. However, the illegal cocaine market keeps the price very high, and coca production has increased dramatically. It is a good way to use one's land to make more money than, say, raising corn or even sheep.

Small business workshop: *On Saturday I gave a workshop on Quaker values in small business education. It was fun pulling it together, mingling my business school marketing training with information from small business workshops I had assisted in Guatemala with indigenous women, and reflecting on Quaker John Woolman's experience in refusing to write contracts to buy and sell people as slaves. We talked about how Quakers have always declined to barter, setting a fair price instead. I shared my experience in the 1980s when I organized the Women's Housing Initiative with Susan Davies and Anne Gelbspan in Boston, and how Cambridge Friends Meeting testified to its values in assisting that organization with a large loan and spiritual support. The participants were interested to hear about a whole community working together to create a project, since most of their work tends to be individually based.*

We had a great time talking about examples of local business decisions. How forty women can sell bread at the same corner by the church, and whether it is likely that all of them will be successful. It is a good example of market competition. We talked about how the microbus drivers can afford to be rude to the customer. There is no need for customer loyalty in that business, since the supply of buses is lower than the demand. We talked about how it is important in a small business to keep your personal funds separate from your business, and to pay the business back if you use items for your family. How important it is not to let the children eat the candy in your store, or to eat the chicken that you are raising for eggs! We talked about some of the microfinance agencies that are sprouting up in Bolivia, and some of the dangers of too much access to credit.

Cochabamba: In our travels through Bolivia, we went to the inauguration of a new Quaker church in Cochabamba, in the lowlands, only 1,000 feet higher than Denver. It is a small congregation called Congregación Cristiana Amigos. On Saturday, we got up at dawn with the pastor and his family to go over to the church and undertake a massive clean-up before it got too hot to work comfortably. The building was built recently, and there were huge piles of construction materials and debris in the yard. The community consisted of only four households and a few friends, so our help was really needed, especially that of my three tall and strong teens. Everybody was amazed at their strength and energy. We piled up a truck-full of trash for pickup out front, sorted and stored good construction materials, and made some steps for the front door. Then we laid carpet and flooring and cleaned the place from top to bottom. It is a lovely building; the Friends have the first floor, consisting of a worship room, kitchen and bath and two classrooms. Under the management of Hans, one of our hosts, they operate a fabulous modern audio-visual system which allows them to project movies onto the wall. Their Quaker religious services are completely wired, a far cry from our silent meetings for worship in New England.

The next day we shared a feeling of exhilaration with the congregation as the sparkling new rooms filled up with Friends and other visitors from the community, joined by supporters from La Paz and Santa Cruz. Many of these Quaker supporters had taken an overnight bus to Cochabamba to celebrate the opening of the new church, having helped in the development of the small Cochabamba Quaker Meeting. Each of the visiting pastors offered impassioned prayers and songs, asking for growth and health for the little church in its new space. I was pleased to hear the beautiful song that our Cuban Friends love so much, "Si no Fuera por Tí" ("If it weren't for you, God, what would have happened to me?")

Friends Ninfa and Hans, Daniel, Freddie and Marta had worked very hard to welcome the visitors. There was a chicken dinner catered and provided for all afterwards. We felt a kinship with this small Quaker meeting as our own Quaker congregation has been this small at various times in the past, and is now blessed with a growing and loving community.

Conor's reflections on Cochabamba:

We stayed in Cochabamba for a few days, the site of the infamous "Water Wars". This happened very recently, when big companies bought the rights to the water supply, and started charging Bolivians to use it. People started rioting and eventually succeeded in getting the companies to leave. A movie was made about this, called "Tambien La Lluvia", "Even the Rain". It is about how the companies would charge even for the rain. We stayed with some Quaker friends in Cochabamba and played with their young son.

From my journal:

Travel by bus: *Bus travel through Bolivia means mountains. Not just the trip down from the Cordillera to Coroico, the so called "death road", considered the most dangerous road in the world. Every trip in western Bolivia involves climbing impossible roads up through the mountains with breathtaking views. Right now we are on the well-traveled route from Cochabamba to La Paz. We are inching along behind a sixteen-wheeler. It is an eight-hour trip, and the second driver is sleeping down below in the sleeping berth, awaiting his turn to drive. We are upstairs, on the second story. The higher level adds to the drama and the views. Evan is sitting in the front seat, perched over the front of the bus. We pass tiny villages of sheep farmers, whose mud brick houses with thatched roofs hug the hillsides. Families are out carrying water and watching their herds. Some have put their laundry out to dry on the rocks: enormous pollera skirts, matching petticoats, and hand-woven blankets with geometric patterns in earth tones. The mountain ranges stretch out to the horizon in all directions. When we pass a town, little kids run to offer us soft drinks from their families' stands. As the sun sinks behind the mountains, the houses blend into the rocks and the doors to the houses are all closed against the cold night air.*

Conor on leaving Bolivia

"Cha-Chunk-Cha-Chunk-Cha-Chunk", the sound of the train tracks running under the aged train. The interior is very dusty, although not because of its age. The tracks sit on very loose, dusty dirt, so the speed flings dust up into the air and it eagerly jumps into the face of anyone sitting next to an open window. As the sun streams in through the window, dodging even the metal washboard blinds, slipping through gaps, the car's temperature begins to rise along with the irresistible urge to just crack open the window, only the tiniest bit. Inevitably, the dust rushes in, just before the wind cools off the inside of the car.

We are heading south towards the Bolivia/Argentina border, leaving Bolivia, our suitcases with us this time, a sign we won't be coming back after two or three weeks. The flat south of Bolivia, contrasting with the mountainous north, whips by, leaving two months of memories behind. Some, like playing ultimate Frisbee with the kids in the Hogar in Sorata, teaching "Head, Shoulders, Knees and Toes" to first graders and sophomores alike, spending long Sunday mornings with Quakers, and many other memories cling to the back of the train, following us towards Argentina, infinity, and beyond.

COMING HOME

People often say it is harder to return from a life-changing trip than it was to leave home in the first place. That was the case for me. Upon my return, I found myself un-tethered from work and community obligations and disconnected from the extravagant way of life in the US. I felt isolated and alone, despite the joy I felt in coming back to my friends, extended family, and my Quaker community. Some of what I missed was the extraordinary physical closeness our family had during the Big Trip. Not many parents have the joy of sharing days and nights with their adolescent offspring, even sleeping as close as puppies in a pile. I remembered the times that Laura and I had shared a bed, including a double bed in a windowless room in Kenya and a very cold and wet tent in the Andes. For a couple of months in Bolivia, the four of us shared a small guest bedroom. We worked on joint projects daily and ate dinner together most nights. When we came back home, I missed the physical closeness, and even more, the camaraderie of being a family team that we had experienced over the year.

My children had the opposite problem: they returned to a structured academic life that was at the same time comforting and chafing. Accustomed to creating their own learning environment, they now had to rely on someone else's structure. We did get used to home life again, big cars, enough hot water and a closet full of clothes. We re-integrated ourselves with our home community, and rebuilt our work and home lives. But the return home was bumpy, as predicted.

A few weeks after I returned home, I woke to an extraordinarily loud noise: power saws just outside my bedroom window. Our new neighbors had decided to cut all the trees down between their property and ours. What had been a leafy bower—albeit filled with junk trees—was turned into a bare expanse, with the only sight outside the windows being our neighbor's home. In one day, the entire experience of living in our home changed from rural to urban, from private and quiet to loud and public. It was a very unhappy time. Facing a denuded yard and a house devoid of kids, I felt I had lost my home.

But as I came to grips with this new stage in my life, I was able to move past the daily changes in my circumstances to reflect on the wisdom we gained as a family from the Big Trip. What did we learn? We learned that home is not a place; it's a feeling of being together. As our kids get older and more independent, we hold dear those memories of our travel time together. Unlike our daily lives at home, when each is in his or her private bubble, meeting up for meals and sometimes little else, we traveled the same circles on the Big Trip. There was time to reflect on what we'd observed in our travels. Time waiting for a city bus or preparing meals together offered us opportunities to share observations and learn things from each other. Sometimes one of the kids would say to me, "Mom, I noticed how you responded to that guy. It sounded sort of rude." Normally at home, I would be too rushed to take in that kind of suggestion from one of my children. How can they help me be a better person? Who are they to say that? But on the Big Trip, I had time to consider. More often than not, their observations were right. Maybe I even became a better person from listening to them! When we volunteered together, we worked as a team for perhaps the first time in our lives. Each of us had our own contributions to make, and we worked as colleagues, setting aside our parental/child roles.

So now, we have the challenge of re-creating those times of togetherness, creating a home together wherever we meet. It may be a meal together on a college campus, or taking a family walk in the woods during a too-short holiday vacation. We know the value of those moments, and we all work to make them happen from time to time as our individual circles get wider. As our children become more independent, those times together are rarer. We are thankful that we were able to delve into a time of togetherness before the moving apart began.

Did our kids give up complaining for good? These kids are not saints. Finding fault, especially with one's parents, is what teens do best. They did not give this up. But they definitely picked up some inner fortitude on our Big Trip, an ability to endure privations without complaint. Perhaps I can say that they grew up. When the food is lacking, or the wind is cold, they are more likely to bear up than to complain. I think this attitude is connected with their new understanding of how most people in the world live lives completely different from our own, and much harder. This understanding will serve them well.

By far, the most important change in our lives upon returning home was a shift in our personal relationship with the world outside the US borders. Our knowledge of people and places in other parts of the world has a new intimacy. The feeling that we are all connected—with people who are far away from us, and whose lives are different from ours—stays with us, and continues to grow along with new connections that we make.

Our teens still carry a feeling of daily life in other cultures. They often write about their experiences abroad when asked to reflect on something in their school work, whether it's the history of Incan warriors, Franco's Spain, or life in East Africa. They have breathed the air of foreign places, and this colors their understanding of those places with more detail. Laura corrects herself in conversation. "I mean we, not they," she says. The same is true for me. When I hear of news from Morocco or Kenya, I understand it more deeply than before. There is a flash of recognition. *Yes, I know people like that. I was on that street. I ate the food they ate. And I'm still learning about those cultures.*

And having learned a bit about what it is like to be Moroccan or Kenyan, my heart will never be able to brush off those stories, those lives, as it might have done before. The suffering I saw in Marrakech is not forgettable. The children posted outside the ice cream shop well past their bedtimes, offering napkins to customers on the way in, and asking for money on the way out—those memories tug at me. The people we met and the friends we made have become a part of my life. I still maintain strong friendships with many of them.

I have found that my work back home takes on a fresh urgency. Perhaps I am not doing more work, but caring more about the work that I choose. I have felt drawn to work that is simultaneously local and also foreign, in what I call "the country no one wants to visit", the criminal justice system. I have started spending time with prisoners through a program that has been in existence since the 1970s, but one that I have only recently had time to enter: the Alternatives to Violence Project. This program helps prisoners to learn methods for resolving conflicts and ultimately helps to build a sacred community within the criminal justice system, with threads running to the volunteers "on the outside". It is work that feeds me both emotionally and spiritually. Spanish-speaking volunteers are particularly needed in this program, for both US and international sites. So along with my day-to-day life, I am finding ways to continue to weave together the threads of community and service.

Father Greg Boyle founded an organization in Los Angeles called Homeboys Industries which works with urban teens at risk. He speaks about the linkage between the concepts of service and community, describing service as "the hallway that leads to the ballroom" of mutuality and kinship. He rightly points out that we are all seeking a sense of connection with others. I love this image of the world as a party, a place where the best work is done with joy and through relationships among people. Volunteers often talk about feeling that they have gained more than they gave. In providing service to others, we forge bonds with others who are different from us, people with whom we thought we had little in common.

Our Big Trip was about forging bonds with others, sometimes in service and sometimes in fellowship. Both types of interactions were rich with mutual sharing. We keep these bonds alive through the miracle of the internet, a tool that is becoming increasingly available worldwide. These threads of relationship connect us with others around the world, bringing caring and hope for the future. "What was your experience in Hurricane Sandy?" "Were the elections peaceful in your village?" "How is your young family?" These conversations continue across the miles on Facebook and email, and the world seems a smaller place than before our journey.

Many people feel that they cannot afford to take a Big Trip. A yearlong vacation, with hotels, restaurant meals and frequent air travel would be beyond the means of most people. However, a Big Trip does not need to include this level of travel. Our natural inclination was towards slow travel with a focus on service and community. This type of trip does not have to cost much. Our entire trip cost under $60,000 for the year, including airfare for the four of us and five visits from home for John. We lived mainly with friends and acquaintances, or in housing provided to volunteers. We cooked and ate our own food for the most part, frequently sharing meals with our hosts, and used public transportation. This sum also included weekend outings and side trips, where we did stay in the occasional hotel or rent a car. We lived a good part of the year in the global south, where costs are much lower.

What people often do not take into account when considering a family gap year is that many of the regular outflows of a household come to a stop. Organized sports, music lessons, frequent shopping trips to buy the latest fashions or sports equipment—all these are unnecessary on a Big Trip. No gasoline or car repairs are needed, nor are expensive restaurants or weekend trips. Freedom from these regular expenses results, as well as much more free time. All these savings should be balanced against the cost of an extended trip. Also, a careful budget can help to anticipate the net cost of a family gap year. If a job or school schedule shortens the trip, the savings will be less as well, and airfare becomes a larger proportion of the total. Yet the same principle applies in keeping costs low.

Our trip was unusual in that one parent continued to work. It takes a special kind of parent and spouse to agree to stay home while his family goes on the adventure of a lifetime. But John is that kind of person. He celebrated the trip as a rare opportunity for his family, although he was only able to be a part-time participant. When one parent stays at home, continuing to pay the mortgage and hold down the tent pegs, the financial risk is much lower. What is forfeited is the opportunity to experience the adventure together as a complete family. We enjoyed having him visit us after we had settled into a location, and we showed him our projects with pride. We made it work. Other families have jobs that are mobile, and can be accomplished from abroad, so that the income continues to flow. Different situations call for various solutions. No one structure works best.

Some would say that instead of spending money on airfare to travel to Europe, Africa, Central and South America, we should have sent the same amount to people who need it. Can we justify travel, from an anti-poverty perspective? And what about the effect of traveling on carbon dioxide levels in the atmosphere? Air travel has a huge impact on global warming. We did limit our plane travel to five flights over the course of the year, in addition to John's occasional trips to visit us. However, the larger question is whether international travel for cultural awareness, even slow travel, is defensible. A good case can be made that it is not. We are doing something selfish that only a small minority of the world's inhabitants can afford to do. In the future, when even less of the world's carbon is left, air travel will probably be seen as an anachronism, an outlandishly selfish habit, long discontinued.

And yet one can never fully anticipate the impact of one's actions. In responses from people we met, we could see that they were glad we had made the trip. We often heard sentiments like this: "I always thought that all Americans drank Coke." "I never thought that there were any Americans not in favor of the war in Iraq…. or Afghanistan." And on foreign language: "I thought that most Americans did not speak a foreign language." By simply showing up and being ourselves, we changed stereotypes, and broadened people's understanding of our culture. Some of what we taught on our journeys was hopefully of some value to others. Our classes in English, silk-screening, and microfinance may have helped to spark a change in someone's life. Even more likely, something we said or did inadvertently might have had a positive impact; it might have encouraged someone to try something they thought they could not do.

To us it seemed that most of the learning that went on was ours. We brought back knowledge and ideas, widespread elsewhere, from which we can learn here in the US. We came home with a deeper understanding of life in other cultures, and the kids brought back detailed understanding of macroeconomics, history, politics and international development. We learned about how other cultures deal with racial diversity, conflicts with neighboring countries, and governmental resource distribution. We learned enough to know that there is far more to learn, and that learning about the world is a lifelong project. As we hoped, we have become citizens—and students—of the world.

I don't expect to resolve this debate about the ultimate value compared with the cost of travel. But in the final analysis, it is not a reason to forgo such a trip. We can always find reasons not to take a jump into the unknown. It's too expensive, we tell ourselves. It is bad for the environment to travel. (But do we think about the toll on the environment when we travel for business, or take the family to Florida for a week?) In my own mind, these concerns are red herrings, hiding the real reason that most of us do not take a leap into a trip such as this: fear. I had a lot of fears before the Big Trip began. Would the kids forget how to go to school—or refuse to? Would something bad happen to us? Would we run out of money? Or my father's concern, given that John would not be with us the entire year, "Your marriage will never survive this." And it does take courage to leap into the unknown, towing your family behind you.

But I can say that once you are on the trip, the fear drops away. Like a turtle, traveling with one's family brings home along with you. I truly felt at home everywhere we traveled. And even though there were multiple uncertainties every step of the way, those we met often welcomed us with open arms and melted away our fears.

I tell our story because I know that people are drawn to travel as to a fascinating book, to learn about others and to feel what life is like in other places. It may or may not be a justifiable expense in the larger scheme of things, but one never knows. Ripples travel far. In traveling and being an active part of the many communities we visited, we helped to weave a web of community worldwide.

As a Quaker, I hold dear the principles that Friends use to guide our paths. These principles do not form a creed, but rather a mirror which we can hold up to question our actions and consider how we are being asked to live, so as to encourage the right ordering of our lives. There are four such principles: Simplicity, Peace, Integrity, and Equality. We learned so much from others during our travels around all of these issues, and what we learned gave rise to questions in our hearts. These are some of the questions that we have been pondering since our return.

Simplicity: What would our lives look like if we reduced our energy consumption and the possessions we own to the level of that of most of the people in the world? How can we move in this direction? Can we reduce our habit of getting more "stuff" just because it is new? Can we occasionally slow down our lives to obtain the refreshment and clarity of mind that we experienced when we walked the Camino for several weeks? How can we introduce that clarity and calm into our everyday lives?

Peace: What can we learn from the experience of Córdoba, the Spanish city where Christians, Jews and Muslims lived in relative peace in the thirteenth and fourteenth centuries, under Mozarabic leadership? What can we learn from the work of Quakers in East Africa, who help victims and perpetrators in the genocides in Burundi and Rwanda to walk with each other, having created a sacred space where forgiveness has taken place? And personally, how can we work towards more peaceful interactions in our daily lives, letting go of the need to be right?

Integrity: How can we travel among others whose values and opinions are very different from ours, listening to their truth while remaining faithful to our own values? How far should we go in asserting our beliefs, as visitors to other cultures? What ideas can we adopt from the example of people whose lives are dedicated to work they believe in, from the Children's Care Center in Kakamega, Kenya to the children's afterschool center, Los Patojos, in Guatemala? How can we make life choices that are more in harmony with our beliefs?

Equality: How can we help to bring to an end the inequality experienced by poor people all over the world, from Mayan villagers in Guatemala to Berber minorities in Morocco? What are we willing to give up to right some portion of the wrongs in our society? Are we willing to listen with open minds to our so-called "enemies", knowing that everyone is given a measure of truth?

Something that became clear to all of us during our travels was the huge separation between the United States and other countries. As a country, we put ourselves on a pedestal, and much of the world sees us as a distant power, unapproachable and dangerous. We are taught to feel both superior and afraid of others, especially of those who lack our power and resources. These feelings have historic and geographic origins. The United States is surrounded by water on east and west, and neighbors on the north and south that do not threaten us. We even call our country "America", blind to the reality of so many others who live on the continent, and perhaps claiming the entire continent, north and south, for ourselves. Unlike Europeans, we cannot travel a few miles to another country where another language is spoken and other laws pertain. Many of us have never traveled outside the country, and this creates a feeling that everything we have is unique and special. Our country was built on the promise of something bigger and better than other places. As a European friend of mine said when she visited, "Everything is bigger in the United States—the cars, the highways, even the land!" The geography of this country and our historical sense of American exceptionalism have created the sense that we have the best of everything and little to learn. Along with that notion comes a fear of others, as indeed much of the world does not have the wealth that we have here.

We have much to be proud of as US citizens, and we can celebrate our good luck to have been born here. But patriotism should not blind us to the wisdom we can learn from others or to an open-eyed assessment of how we can improve our country. We certainly do not have all the answers; we could benefit tremendously as a nation by asking more questions of and learning from other countries.

I am convinced that we will never have security in our country until we work to bring justice to others. Others have much to teach us in reducing our use of the world's resources. Simply put, we must consume less. And if we don't do so voluntarily, we will eventually be forced to. For example, as gas prices continue their inexorable rise, world demand will soon surpass peak oil availability, if it has not done so already. Then we will slide down the supply curve to where oil is increasingly expensive and difficult to extract, leaving us with no choice but to search for alternative solutions.

Likewise, we must learn to stop building weapons and to find ways to communicate with other nations beyond threatening violence. Worldwide, we need to be more of a friend and less of a bully.

My vision for a peaceful world is described in the Song of Peace, a hymn written in 1934 by Lloyd Stone for the Finlandia Hymn melody composed by Jean Sibelius.

But other lands have sunlight too and clover, and skies are everywhere as blue as mine.

Other lands with sunlight too, have solutions for many of the world's problems. We would do well to listen respectfully to these ideas. Many people across the world who hold themselves to the highest ideals and demonstrate the highest human talents live with far fewer resources than we do, and they have found ingenious solutions to the world's many problems. The American dream is not everyone's dream. Europeans, Africans and South Americans—all have their own dreams for their societies, including standards for the right way to live.

When we travel, we see clearly the choices governments and people make in their use of resources. Innovative solutions are all around us. We could learn from them: how to access from your tap hot water, heated instantaneously on demand instead of being held continuously in a fifty gallon tank in the basement, or how to encourage private bus services in order to reduce the number of private automobiles needed. We saw simple energy-saving programs like the one used in most hotels across Europe, in which the electric power for each room is connected to its key card. Living without heat or air conditioning and washing dishes in cold water expanded our notions of acceptable temperatures in the home.

Though our family has returned to a profligate use of central heating, gasoline, and other resources, we are more aware of our use of resources than before our Big Trip. We have all found ways to use fewer resources in our daily lives, such as hanging clothes out to dry instead of using the clothes drier and using less water while washing dishes. We have put solar panels on our roof, turning our home into a mini-electricity factory. We use less plastic. All of us buy fewer clothes than before. Evan lives the most simply of all of us, choosing to own very few possessions, taking public transportation almost exclusively, and living "off the grid" in the mountains every summer, working with the Appalachian Mountain Club trail crew. All around us, people are living with a greater sense of environmental awareness, striving to live more responsibly. The crisis of climate change is becoming clearer to many in our society, as it has been clear for some time in Europe and other countries.

If we are to survive here on Planet Earth, we all need to work together on these problems and learn from each others' solutions. Bolivia's groundbreaking law of protection for Mother Earth, or Pachamama, the earth goddess and creator of all in the indigenous Aymara tradition, offers new strategies for environmental protection. Because of this legislation, lawsuits can be brought claiming damages to Pachamama. An entire nation has recognized the earth's rights. We could use this helpful frame of reference here in the United States. Bolivians are keenly aware of climate change since the glaciers in western Bolivia, reservoirs of drinking waters for the inhabitants of that country, have diminished thirty percent in the last two decades.

Indigenous Bolivians see clearly the link between their spirituality and the planet's sustainability. To live in harmony on the earth requires protection of its resources to create a home for future generations. Likewise, my Quaker faith asks me to simplify my life, to use fewer resources, and not to take more than my share. I started out on a courageous journey, a journey of love for my family. I arrived home with a heart full of compassion, more aware of the struggles faced by people in other parts of the world and more appreciative of the lessons that can be learned from our neighbors.

TWO YEARS LATER

In the early fall, two years after our Big Trip, John and I find ourselves walking the Camino again. This time we are walking without the children, since they are all in school. It is our first vacation alone together in 21 years, traveling as we used to travel before the children were born. It is a time to build new patterns, to remember who we are besides being parents, a role that has been central to our understanding of ourselves for a generation. Now our children do not need us as often, and we have become weekly parents, instead of daily or hourly parents as we were before.

Walking the Camino gives us time to feel our way into this new role, to walk into our future with intention. It is an amazing opportunity to be able to re-order our priorities and our time. We have found that there is much more time on our hands when we don't have to prepare three meals a day, every day. We bot•h have time to branch out in new directions, together and apart. On the Camino, we talk together about our new lives, about what interests us, and about our futures. Unlike at home, where we often feel like two trains on parallel tracks, we have time to be with each other, and time to walk alone, knowing the other is nearby but not needing to interact.

John on the Camino

Walking the Camino gives us time to feel our way into this new role, to walk into our future with intention. It is an amazing opportunity to be able to re-order our priorities and our time. We have found that there is much more time on our hands when we don't have to prepare three meals a day, every day. We bot•h have time to branch out in new directions, together and apart. On the Camino, we talk together about our new lives, about what interests us, and about our futures. Unlike at home, where we often feel like two trains on parallel tracks, we have time to be with each other, and time to walk alone, knowing the other is nearby but not needing to interact.

We interact more with other walkers, without our family bubble around us. I wonder what we missed when we were engrossed in family conversations the last time we were here. I hope we weren't too loud. This time, the rhythm of the Camino absorbs us early on. Our first evening, we share a meal family-style with the other walkers staying in an albergue perched on the very edge of the Pyrenees. Our hosts ask us to introduce ourselves. The first brave soul begins haltingly, mentioning his name, hometown and country. Soon we are hearing about celebrations, relationships, and hopes that the body will hold up through the long walk. We hear French, Spanish and English spoken, each according to the language in which s/he feels most comfortable. I offer a few words in French, since we are in fact in France. The process of creating a community has begun.

As the days go by, we often cross paths with these same travelers. Some walk slower or faster than we, and we do not see them again. But we see many of them along the way. A striking woman from Sweden had the fashion sense to pack a long flowing dress for evening wear in her pack, saying she prefers to wear dresses in the evening. We see her stopping for coffee on a cool, foggy slope near the top of the mountains, wearing a much more practical windbreaker and rain pants. We meet two brothers-in-law from France, who have walked a full month before arriving at the official start of the Camino on the French/Spanish border. They tell us about the beauty of the earlier stages of the Camino that wind through southern France. Already we have our next Camino planned, a hoped-for future trip.

We meet other interesting people along the way. A young Asian man who is a Marist Brother tells us about his relationship with the Church and his disagreements with Church policy. He must have an amazing amount of optimism and patience. He impresses me with his openness to other people's lives and opinions. He would be a wonderful friend, and we share email addresses, hoping to welcome him to our home when he comes to New England for a conference. Later, we meet Natalie, a fast walker from New Zealand who has fallen into conversation with Hugo, an economics professor from Holland. They are having an animated conversation about globalization and third world poverty, Natalie's concentration in her recent university program. Hugo is a smoker, so I am surprised to see them still together that evening, hanging out their laundry on lines at a guest house in a nearby village.

A fancy meal on the Camino

We take shortcuts and long cuts, because we are only two. We eat more meals in restaurants. We travel to an ancient monastery that still has remains of its Visigothic, Moorish, Romanesque and

Gothic architectural history. It is a little gem the size of a summer cottage, perched on the side of a mountain. This building's bones have been here for 1500 years. After this long cut, we cheat and take a bus along the route to catch up to where we need to be in order to make it to Burgos on time for our plane home. The bus covers a day's walk in twenty minutes. We feel chagrined to see how fast we cover the ground that would have taken us at least six hours. The bus route parallels the Camino, and we duck as we pass some of our new friends.

A frequent conversation-opener on the Camino is: "How heavy is your pack?" Woe betide the person who has packed too much stuff, and loses the friendly competition to be the one who has packed lightest. Simplicity is admired on the Camino! Or alternatively, envy is reserved for those who purchased the lightest, newest, most expensive trekking attire. Unfortunately, I over-packed this time around. I was too busy prior to the trip and as a result, I tossed too many items into my pack instead of carefully considering each one. When I realized that I had brought along three heavy jack knives, as well as unneeded sweaters and mittens, we found a post office and sent them home. Once again, I learned the lesson: less stuff is better.

Spain seems to be worse off economically than last time we were here. Three years ago, we were offered many gifts along the trail: a basket of fresh plums left invitingly for us to help ourselves, or freshly made jam. This time there are no gifts, and many of the young people we meet are walking because they have nothing else to do. It is September, and they want to be doing something. There are many worse choices. But many of their stories are sad. Surprisingly, there is little panhandling on the Camino, and not much theft. Only a few times do we see people who take the opportunity to ask the pilgrims for money. One man did set up a table on the side of the trail with food and drinks for sale, and a big sign asking for help. Perhaps asking pilgrims for alms is not a successful business plan.

The sense of history is always present along the Camino. When we arrive at a narrow pass in the mountains, heading down into France, we see a wonderful story carved into stone. Someone has written an imaginative essay about people who have passed this way over the centuries; for example, the knight Roland blew his horn here to let Charlemagne know that he was mortally wounded and needed help. The famous epic poem, "The Song of Roland", was written about his journey; it is the oldest surviving work of French literature. Elisabeth of Valois also traveled this path. As a teenager, she traveled by carriage through the pass to join her future husband, Phillip II of Spain. The marriage offered Spain for a short time a claim to the French throne during the 16th century, the time of Spain's highest ascent on the world stage. Partisans on both sides of the two world wars traveled this route by foot, as did many centuries of traveling Basques, whose ancient language spans the French and Spanish sides of the border. As we walk, we imagine the people who went before us on this path, carrying their hopes and dreams, fears and desires. We feel a kinship with earlier travelers, on our own journeys through life.

Since we were last on the Camino, a new piece of history has been created. In widening the road, a mass grave was discovered, bodies dumped by Franco's troops during the Civil War in the 1930s. On the windy hillside, a monument has been erected to honor the dead. The monument reads: "Their killings were in vain, but their lives were not." We stop to mourn these strangers, and share their plot of ground for a time. This remnant of history, too, is in process. Other families living nearby are still mourning, waiting all these decades later for a sense of closure, for an opportunity to finally put their loved ones' bones to rest. The sense of living history continues right up to this day.

One thing that has not changed since our earlier trip is the blackberries. They are everywhere along the trail. They taste like golden sun and warm earth, combined into fall's sweetest harvest. Taking a blackberry break becomes one of the pleasures of the walk, an energy boost and a boost to the spirits. I remember that when we were last here, I could not convince Laura to keep walking when she had found a patch of delicious berries to munch on.

As a child, my siblings and I picked blackberries along the sides of the road and in untamed and abandoned places. Adding a little lemon juice and a lot of sugar to the berries, my mother made wonderful pies. It was the only time we were allowed to lick our plates clean, and none of us turned down the invitation. I reach for a berry, and time slips away. I am a child on a warm day in early fall, a mother walking the trail with her three teenagers, and an adult alone, leaning into a joyful future.

APPENDIX I: LOGISTICAL SUGGESTIONS

Planning ahead: A traveler with a stronger constitution than I might have chosen not to plan the trip ahead of time, to leave way for chance encounters and luck. I planned ahead. I might have left more to chance if I did not have three teens under my wing. I suspect that planning also suits my personality, and having some certainties provided me with a way to reduce my pre-travel anxiety. I had purchased plane tickets in advance, and decided how much time to spend living in each location. Detailed decisions such as renting an apartment and deciding where to volunteer among several choices were made on the ground. We always avoided guided tours and chose our own route, and we were never unhappy with this choice. I made frequent use of the Rick Steves books on Europe, as well as the excellent *A Pilgrim's Guide to the Camino de Santiago* by John Brierley. In the global south, my preference was divided between the *Lonely Planet Country Guides*, the *Moon Handbooks*, and the *Rough Guides*. On the other hand, sometimes the only way is to strike out on your own, without plans or guidebooks. We took many short trips from our bases in each country that were entirely unplanned, some as long as a week. We could not have found these without local word of mouth, and they were some of our best experiences.

Home sharing: We often travel with an organization called intervac-homeexchange.com. This organization operates the original home exchange service and is a great program for any kind of home or family exchange. Our family has been a member for twenty years and we have had nothing but good experiences with our exchanges, acting both as hosts and as guests. In fact, I've never heard of anyone who had a negative experience with this program. People trust each other to take good care of each other's homes, and they do. Even teenage family members find home stays in other countries in this way. We've had over a dozen exchanges so far. Many of the friends with whom we stayed in Europe on the Big Trip were strangers before we met via Intervac. In addition to this organization, there are many other home exchange organizations, including homexchange.com and couchsurfing. net. Other similar programs have a more direct focus on cultural exchange, including Servas International, which was founded in 1949, with the motto *Peace through Understanding*. Many people whose interest is in organic farming stay at farms where they are offered room and board in exchange for farming help. The best-known organization in this area is World Wide Opportunities on Organic Farms (WWOOF).

Telephone service: The best way to make local calls abroad is to buy a cheap cell phone in the United States or abroad and make sure it is an "unlocked quad phone". The US telephone market has strong economic interests in preventing US customers from unlocking their phones, though in other countries the unlocked phone is standard. We found a Verizon employee who was willing to walk us through the unlocking process over the phone. I think he was sitting under his desk at the time. For a few bucks, one can buy a SIM card in country, for making calls from that country. Cell phone time can be purchased at corner stores and programmed into the phone. Generally the small children who help out their parents at corner stores are adept at this job. Cell phones are becoming ubiquitous around the world and can be purchased in larger towns everywhere. Traveling with one's cell phone from home runs the risk of inadvertent roaming charges which can run up thousands of dollars. If traveling with one's own phone from home, be sure to put the plan on hold while traveling, and buy a local plan instead. To make long distance phone calls while traveling, Skype offers excellent service for international as well as domestic calls. We generally turned off the visual aspect for better connectivity in the global south.

Computer use: It is helpful to have a relatively inexpensive computer while traveling. Internet access is available in every country, though connections are often poor in rural areas. In those areas, especially, internet cafes are good locations for connectivity. Failing that, we have been known to "borrow" connectivity in short visits to hotel lobbies. (We eat something in the restaurant to make our visits legit.) We brought along netbooks that we had purchased in the United States for about $200 each. Without my netbook, I never would have realized that someone had stolen my bank account information in Guatemala, and the loss might have been catastrophic.

Packing: We packed light, with about a week's worth of clothing which we washed often by hand. It was a good exercise in simplicity, and put us in the company of local people doing the same. Warm clothes are heavier and bulkier than summer clothes, so occasionally we were chilly. If changing climates or clothing needs, it is good to consider sending clothing or heavy items such as hiking duds home. We generally used small rolling suitcases and found these to work well everywhere except for hiking, where we used frame packs. Clothing can be stored in train or bus stations for relatively short durations, or sent home when no longer needed. For longer storage, we prevailed on trusted innkeepers (in Europe) or kind Intervac exchange families to store our unneeded possessions.

Food and water: Many people get sick when they travel, and we were struck down occasionally by intestinal viruses. We kept healthy most of the time by eating conservatively and following some basic rules: don't eat anything raw or undercooked, and don't eat too much. Viruses are dose-related, and eating what you need for sustenance but not to excess limits the opportunities for serious infection. As to cut-up fruit or vegetable salad: there is lots of time to enjoy salads when you get home. (The inside of the pineapple is fine to eat, but was it washed prior to cutting? And how clean was the knife? Cooked food is a safer bet.) As for water, we took care to carry our own water bottle and to fill it up wherever bottled water was available. Now that we are not using plastic bottles at home, we are used to carrying our bottles around with us as we did in infancy!

Cheap flights: There are not many opportunities here. They say that purchasing tickets on Tuesday or Wednesday is the best for lower prices, but the prices seem high every day of the week. One route we have used is to purchase tickets through one of the cause-related travel agencies, such as MTS Travel. These companies specialize in non-profit and religious travel. One advantage of these companies is that one can talk to a live agent, a dying breed in the declining travel agency market. Travel and health insurance can be purchased through these companies as well. Another option is to sign up for a new credit card that offers free miles, or to use frequent flyer miles for travel. However, these cards often have restrictions that make them hard to use.

Land travel: In Europe, a family of more than three will find that a rental car is more economical than public transportation, unfortunately. The reverse math holds in the global south, and other disadvantages of car rental in those countries encourage public transportation as well (cars are targets for theft, and lack of road safety makes driving a challenge in much of the world). We never had a problem with public buses and trains. Much of the world has not yet jettisoned public transport, and cheap, safe and frequent carriers are available.

Cash: This is a difficult issue for travelers. Banks cannot be used for debit card withdrawals unless one has an account at that bank, and ATM machines are bugged in much of the global south.

Travelers' checks have gone the way of the dodo bird. We typically used credit cards with merchants, making sure to use a card that had no fee for international use (my Capital One business card offers this service). Some credit card companies offer a prepaid and reloadable card that can be used for merchant payments. However, for obtaining cash there is often little choice but to bring US dollars from home. Wiring is an expensive alternative as is obtaining a cash advance on a credit card. Receiving occasional visitors from home (spouses or others) who can serve as a courier is helpful. Of course the funds must be carefully guarded (we divided them into separate caches in case one was stolen) and the bills must be crisp and clean in order to be accepted for exchange at many foreign banks. Many banks require brand new bills.

Isic.com: This site offers an international student and teacher identity card which is helpful in Europe as well as Latin America for reduced museum rates and some tourist tickets. Membership is inexpensive and also includes codes which can be used for emergency phone calls. Surprisingly, some parts of the world still make use of pay telephones. And those that don't often have telephone services where one can make calls for a fee.

Negotiating prices: Fixed prices are not common in the global south. Travelers can choose to feel as if they are being taken advantage of and harassed at every turn. Or they can choose to see that negotiation is a way of ensuring the merchant's survival, and realize that the local currency is generally much more valuable to the seller than to the tourist buyer. There is no need to find the lowest possible price that a merchant will accept. Paying a higher price may allow the merchant to feed her family that day. This attitude helps to reduce the stress of the market process. We even came to enjoy these interactions, finding ways to joke and relax with merchants, celebrating our common humanity.

Volunteering: Volunteer organizations are everywhere, and they can help volunteers find a way to pitch in easily. But how can one best assess which organization to work with? Some US-based organizations help to bridge this gap by welcoming volunteers from the United States, serving as a volunteer broker and in some cases as a tour group. These organizations charge a substantial fee for their work, and in return they place volunteers, keep them safe, respond to any problems that arise, and ease transitions to and from home. They create a home away from home. For some young people, this is money well spent. If illness or accident strikes, many families prefer to have an international organization to turn to. In particular, teenagers traveling alone might benefit from an organized program. Depending on the travelers, however, this assistance may or may not be necessary. There are plenty of young people who contact NGOs abroad via email or Skype and volunteer for them directly, without the oversight of a special volunteer support agency. We chose the more independent route, and we are glad that we did so. Following is a list of organizations that we recommend:

Guatemala:

- Los Patojos, Jocotenango (near Antigua): an after-school program for children and teens
- Ventanas Abiertas (Open Windows), Las Dueñas (near Antigua): an after-school and tutoring program for children and adults
- Namaste Direct, Antigua: microenterprise training for women
- Proyecto Lingüístico Francisco Marroquín (Antigua): our favorite Spanish language school in Guatemala
- Pop Wuj Language School, Quetzaltenango: a language school and community center that also fosters connections with many volunteer efforts including Dave and Kathy Smith from Canada who visit regularly and run the stove-building project, Safe Stoves
- Long Way Home, Comalapa: an organization that builds schools, community centers and other buildings using sustainable methods including recycled materials
- WINGS, Antigua: an NGO that provides education and training on reproductive health

- Safe Passages, Guatemala City: an NGO that provides opportunities for children working and living in the city garbage dump

Kenya:

- Children's Care Centre, Kakamega: an orphanage for children affected by AIDS
- Amesbury for Africa, Esabalu: sister community with Amesbury, Massachusetts. Programs include water systems, a health clinic and microenterprise training

Bolivia:

- Bolivian Quaker Education Fund, La Paz: An NGO that provides university-level sponsorships in La Paz and support of the Hogar residence in Sorata

Worldwide:

- World Wide Opportunities on Organic Farms (WWOOF): a program where individuals and families offer farming help in return for room and board

- Workaway, a worldwide exchange program where travelers of all ages offer various types of volunteer work in exchange for room and board; minimum stay is one month. Their website states that services range from: "painting to planting, building to babysitting and shopping to shearing".

APPENDIX II:
FRESHMAN TALKS

After we had settled into our daily lives again, I asked the kids to reflect on what the Big Trip had meant to them, and on how it had affected their lives since their return. I kept asking the same question from time to time, but I never got back any clear response. It's hard for anyone, especially teenagers, to distance themselves enough from their lives at any moment to define how they have changed.

But then Conor and Laura were each asked to give a freshman year talk in high school. Neither John nor I had any input on their choice of topic or their presentations. After their speeches were written, however, we were allowed to see them. Each had chosen to write about the gap year. I include these two essays so as to give the youngest the last word.

Conor:

Picture yourself in a small room in Guatemala as a group of curious ten year-olds wait in hesitant awe for what game you'll play with them next. You look down at the cards in your hands, and start to explain.

Merriam-Webster defines volunteerism as the "art or practice of doing volunteer work in a community service." Here at this school, which values the impressive community service rate of its student body, we take volunteering seriously. We frequently send buses to the Greater Boston Food Bank, and students travel to Belize to provide community service. In the last year, my family and I took a gap year, sort of a sabbatical from work and school. Among other things that we did, we spent 6 months volunteering in Guatemala and Bolivia, teaching English and helping in after-school programs. Today, I'll be talking to you about how my personal experience helped me understand volunteering and why we do it.

Throughout history, we humans have had the capacity to empathize with someone less fortunate, to volunteer our time and effort to reach out and help. There are many reasons to volunteer. Some volunteer because of their religion, others to educate themselves about culture or language. Some seem to be motivated solely by altruism, to simply help, without getting anything in return.

Personally, I volunteered from a cultural standpoint, to share ideas and traditions, to teach, but also to learn. We taught English every day for almost a month in a small Bolivian town, and then for a few weeks in the capital, La Paz. For younger students, we sang songs like "Head, Shoulders, Knees and Toes." For high school seniors, we helped with English conversations. While we spent our time teaching, we were also becoming friends with teenagers our own age. Sometimes we trap ourselves into thinking that because we give to others, they can give nothing in return, but most times this is definitely not the case. Our Bolivian friends not only helped us practice our Spanish, but invited us to go downtown to the movies and hang out with them.

An Australian aborigine named Lilla Watson once said, "If you are coming to help me, you are wasting your time. If you are coming because your liberation is bound up with mine, then let us work together." This quote refers to the cooperation needed to be successful, that everyone has a part to play, and we must all play our parts together. We must all work as equals to rectify the injustices we find in the world.

There are so many places that need help, but they are definitely not helpless, nor are they hopeless. In Guatemala, we took a side trip to a city called Quetzaltenango. We visited a non-profit organization that provided the materials to make environmentally friendly stoves, instead of cooking with fire on the kitchen floor. The building process involved leveling the floor, and setting in cinderblocks. We took out the shovels, and started to work, but were soon interrupted by the mother of the family we were helping. She conveyed her interest to help, and we gave her a shovel. She worked quickly and fervently, and before we noticed, she had almost dug too deep a hole. Although she and her family lacked materials and some building expertise, she certainly did not lack energy. It seemed as if she was just waiting for this opportunity to come along, and she didn't necessarily need our help as much as she needed us to bring supplies and direction. It was clear that day that she was very grateful for what we had collectively done, and as we left, there were only smiles about the new stove. Now although we only spent a day working with this organization, we managed to build and complete an energy efficient, safe stove with the help of the family. We didn't have to know anybody, or spend a long time with them; we were able to make a definite and tangible difference in a very short time.

During our two-week stay in Kenya, we spent four days in an AIDS orphanage. This meant we couldn't spend a lot of time with the kids, but we were able to bring plenty of materials to make those four days as fun for them as possible. For example, we brought a suitcase full of crafts such as spinning tops, paints, Frisbees, and a new soccer ball. There's a chance that the kids with whom we shared such a wonderful week don't distinguish us from other volunteers who visited, and this brings up an interesting point. Is what we did there in Kenya helpful, even if they might not remember us? Was it worth it to brighten their day for just a short time? In my opinion, what we did was definitely helpful, definitely worth it. In a day to day sense, we may have given them an extra bit of joy in their life. But also in the big picture, because we volunteered, we were able to spread awareness of this orphanage with our stories back here at home.

I've talked to you today about my unusual gap year experience, but there are plenty of opportunities close to home. All you have to do is spend some time at the food bank, or help pick up trash in a local park. So if you ever find yourself bored over the summer, or during break, just head over to a local soup kitchen. With the right giving attitude, you can't go wrong. I'll leave you with this quote by G. Thomas Gale: *"A pessimist, they say, sees a glass of water as being half empty; an optimist sees the same glass as half full. But a giving person sees a glass of water and starts looking for someone who might be thirsty."*

-Thank You-

Laura:

How many times a day do you flip on a faucet or press a button and miraculously receive a glass of water, a drenched toothbrush, or a shower? Yet how many times a day do we actually take note of water, mind how much we use, or investigate where it comes from? Last year, instead of going to school, I traveled to a few different places around the world and found out just how much I, as a citizen of the United States, consumed, not only in terms of water, but in terms of all the world's resources. In this talk, through stories from three different places I visited last year, I'm going to explore the questionable necessity of most of the developed world's consumer culture, the absurdity of the consumption of this culture when compared to the poverty of the developing world, and the indirect consequences this culture might have on the environment.

After eighth grade graduation, my mom, my two brothers, and I took off work and school for nine months to travel, volunteer, and live simply, kind of like a gap year. For the first two and a half weeks of our trip, we walked the Camino de Santiago, a pilgrimage that spans the width of Spain. Because people come from all over the world to walk the Camino, I was surprised by how quickly a community developed among us, all united by the identity of being a "pilgrim", the name given to walkers. We were all traveling the same route and staying in the same low-cost hostels established exclusively for the use of the "pilgrims", so we got to know the people who were walking at our pace.

One day, we met a 17-year-old kid named Sander who was walking the Camino alone. My 18-year-old brother started talking with him, and Sander ended up traveling with my family for about a week. After that week, I found that I knew more about Sander than I knew about many of the people I had gone to school with every day for the past two years. Walking the Camino, we didn't have anything to distract us or separate us from the surrounding community: no iPods, televisions, or computers, no worries about how we looked or what we were wearing. With only the small amount of material items that would fit in a backpack, we could focus our time on the people around us, and develop much more valuable and less superficial relationships than we had at home. This experience got me wondering how much more "stuff" beyond our basic needs was actually beneficial to our lives and overall happiness.

But what if people's basic needs aren't being met? Then the question turns from whether or not it's necessary to have all this stuff to whether or not it's just. The first time I really had to confront that degree of poverty was when we traveled to Kenya in December. One of the places we visited in Kenya was the "Kakamega Care Center", an orphanage for children whose parents had died due to the AIDS epidemic that has ravaged the country for decades. The total amount of possessions each child owned usually consisted of two sets of clothes and a blanket which could easily fit into a small backpack. During the four days we volunteered with them, they were packing up these possessions and preparing to go to whatever homes they had for Christmas break. For some this meant staying with aunts, uncles, or grandparents, while for others it just meant an empty house. Whatever the destination, when the staffers at the care center wished the children "good luck" on their Christmas vacation, they literally meant it, knowing that the homes the children were returning to could be incredibly unsafe and unreliable. What would the kids I met at the care center think of my home, cluttered with possessions I'll never use? How would they feel if they knew that my family owned not just one car, but two relatively new automobiles? Now, whenever I think of the stark difference in wealth between our two cultures, I feel unhappy, knowing that I'm continuing my daily life of consumption instead of using my resources to help those in need.

When we visited Bolivia, I felt that feeling all over again. We stayed for a month in a small city called Sorata, situated high up in the Bolivian mountains, where we taught English and stayed in a boarding house for high school kids who live too far away from the city to commute to and from school every day. Instead of getting their water from a reservoir or a well, the source of Sorata's water is the river that runs by the city. This river flows directly from a glacier higher up the mountain, one that has for years slowly melted away during the summer, and then frozen up again during the winter. But as global temperatures are rising, the glacier is shrinking. Eventually, the citizens' only source of water will vanish. This is an example of the United Nations Development Program's statement, as reported by the New York Times: "By mid-century, the development of the poorest countries will be halted or even reversed if bold steps are not taken to forestall the effects of climate change." These forecasted changes in our climate will be due to our thirty-minute showers, our foods imported by air, our dishwashers, laundry machines, heaters and air conditioners to name just a few, all of which add carbon dioxide to the air and contribute to the melting of Sorata's glacier. The United States, however, must take a large part of the blame for the melting of the glacier since, according to www.CO2now.org and www.worldatlas.com, we are the second biggest carbon dioxide polluter in the world. We are second only to China, whose population is 1.3 billion people, whereas our population is only 300 million. In this way, our consumer culture not only perpetuates the unequal distribution of wealth and resources, but also destroys the environment.

However, we can look to Bolivia for leadership on this issue. Although Bolivia is not at all the root cause of the disturbing changes in our climate, its government has nevertheless taken steps to combat climate change, reports the British newspaper, The Guardian. Last spring, Bolivia passed laws that enable lawsuits to be brought to court claiming damages to "Mother Earth" or "Pachamama," the creator of life in the indigenous Aymara tradition. This sense of responsibility for the ultimate effects of human actions is what I believe might be lacking in our culture of consumerism, and what I think will be necessary if we want to avoid the worst effects of climate change.

Through traveling with my family last year, I gained perspective on the harmful consequences of the consumerism that is so inherent in our culture. First, its superficiality limits our ability to build strong communities. Second, it is unjust in the face of the poverty abundant in the world, and third, it contributes largely to the destruction of our climate. However, I have to say that I feel hypocritical standing here and delivering this message, when I have willingly and happily participated in consumerism all my life. But perhaps if we shift away from a culture that values consumption to one that values its communities and each individual's responsibility for those communities, we may be able to build a more connected, more socially conscious and more environmentally secure future. Thank you.